BREAKTHROUGH

Also co-authored by Donald Cowper and Andrew Haynes

. . . .

Youth Violence: How To Protect Your Kids

BREAKTHROUGH

Take Your Business and Sales to the Top

David Cowper

with Donald Cowper & Andrew Haynes

HiGHRiSE
B O O K S

BREAKTHROUGH:
TAKE YOUR BUSINESS AND SALES TO THE TOP

A Highrise Book

Published by DNA Creative
621 Milverton Blvd., Toronto, Ontario, M4C 1X8, Canada

Cowper, David
Breakthrough: Take Your Business and Sales to the Top

ISBN 0-9682030-0-0
copyright © 1997 by DNA Creative

Design by Late Harvest Entertainment

Printed and bound in Canada

ABOUT THE AUTHORS

David Cowper

David Cowper, CLU, has been in the insurance business for 39 years. He is among the highest performing insurance brokers in the world and a founding member of the Top of the Table. He speaks around the globe and has been a Main Platform speaker for the Top of the Table and the Million Dollar Round Table. He is a former member of the Faculty of Life Underwriters Association, former member of the Directors of Life Underwriters Association, and former Chairman of the Taxation and Legislation Committee of Life Underwriters Association of Canada. He is a tenor, an avid reader of history, and an aficionado of thoroughbred horse racing. He lives with his wife, Teri, in Toronto.

Donald Cowper

Donald Cowper, a former insurance broker, is now a writer, and co-author with Kevin Guest and Andrew Haynes of *Youth Violence: How To Protect Your Kids*. He lives in Toronto with his girlfriend and editor, Ann Margaret.

Andrew Haynes

Andrew Haynes, former publisher of *The Species Review*, a Canadian high-tech magazine, is a writer and co-author of *Youth Violence: How To Protect Your Kids*. He lives in Toronto with his wife, Christine.

Acknowledgments

For nearly 20 years, people have been asking me where my book is. I would always reply, "It's coming – soon." Now, thanks to the help of my son Donald and Andrew Haynes, I can at last say that it is here.

I am indebted to Ann Margaret Oberst for her expert editing, Christine Rooney for her insightful suggestions, and my daughter, Dara Cowper, for her astute comments. However, I take full responsibility for any errors that still remain in the book.

Thanks to Leonid Rozenberg for his inspired design of this book.

Deep thanks go to my wife, Teri, for all her support and love and advice on the manuscript.

I must also thank my other sons, David Jr. and Dalton, and my partner, Richard Steyn, for their input and encouragement.

Donald and Andrew would like to extend their heartfelt thanks to Ann Margaret and Christine for all of their encouragement, love and invaluable assistance throughout the many long days of this project.

David Cowper
April 24, 1997

To Teri, who has always been the wind beneath my wings.

"He either fears his fate too much

Or his deserts are small,

That puts it not unto the touch,

To win or lose it all."

James Graham, Marquis of Montrose
(1612-1650), to his mistress

BREAKTHROUGH

In this book, I outline the strategies I have developed during my career to take my business and sales to the top. I am an insurance broker, but the strategies are universal, applicable to all fields and all businesses.

Throughout this book, I sometimes refer to products, concepts, and laws that may or may not apply to your particular area.

All the cases I describe in this book are based on real events, however, in order to protect the privacy and confidentiality of my clients, I have changed all their names and all the telling details of the stories. I have also changed the names of everyone else in this book, except for my own, and those of my wife, Teri, and my first manager in the business, the late Huss Breithaupt. I have also not referred to any particular insurance companies, except the company where I first learned to sell: The New York Life Insurance Company.

CONTENTS

PART I
The $100,000,000 case

1. The $100,000,000 conversation   21

PART II
*How to lay the foundation for taking
your business to the top*

2. Creative survival in the lean years   29
3. The knowledge breakthrough   55
4. The power of passion   67
5. Meet the people   79
6. Understand your prospects   95

PART III
*How to sell megacases and take your
business to the top*

7. Preparation: the Process Approach   115
8. The sales meeting: turning prospects into clients   135
9. Persistence in the megacase   153

PART IV
How to become a mega-agent

10. Visualization   179
11. The mega-agent   191

PART V
Beyond the megacase

12. A one-billion-dollar year   209

PART I

The $100,000,000 case

At 7:15 it would all be over.

There were two possible results:

I would either realize

my dream, or it would vanish.

Either way,

my life would be

forever changed.

CHAPTER I

The $100,000,000 conversation

I passed the turnoff for the highway and slowed down, easing my car onto the shoulder, the tires crunching gravel. It was 6:45 AM and the traffic was light, but steady – brief intervals of silence punctuated by the occasional rush of a car roaring past. I hadn't had much sleep, but my nerves kept me awake. Fifteen minutes to go, and as the seconds ticked away my heart rate accelerated. I needed to relax; everything would depend on my ability to stay focused, controlled. At 7:15 it would all be over. There were two possible results: I would either realize my dream, or it would vanish. Either way, my life would be forever changed.

I looked ahead through the windshield, my eyes following the lines of the highway to the vanishing point, where I fixed my gaze. Everything else – the panorama of cars, clouds, low-lying buildings – began to undulate like a large tapestry. The traffic sounds faded. I closed my eyes, and meditated. I felt myself relaxing, my mind clearing. When I opened my eyes, I glanced at the clock. It was 6:59. He would arrive any second now, and I was ready.

In the rear-view mirror, I caught a glimpse of a long, black limousine. It approached stealthily like a submarine, passed me, then pulled onto the shoulder. My heart jumped, and I slowly inhaled a deep breath to regain my calm. I reached for the slim leather briefcase on the passenger seat then got out of the car.

The morning air was crisp. I marched over to the right side of the limo, and stood there. I could see his imposing silhouette in the back seat. I had met him only twice before in person. He was a massive man, not overweight, just massive – over six feet tall with a broad face, and deep blue eyes beneath a prominent brow. The driver's door clicked open and a small mustachioed man got out and padded around the car. He walked slowly, or so it seemed. It was like everything was happening in slow motion. I looked down at my watch and gazed as the second hand paused then stuttered forward, paused then stuttered forward again. An eternity later, the driver opened the back passenger door for me and ushered me inside.

I slid along the cool leather, and settled into the seat beside him. "Good morning, Rolf," I said, reaching for a handshake.

He snatched my hand, tugged at it quickly, "You have fifteen minutes."

I opened the clasps on my briefcase and removed a set of six proposals, each one a variation on a $2,000,000 insurance policy. As far as Rolf was concerned that was why I wanted to meet with him – to discuss the $2,000,000 proposal. In truth, I had an ulterior motive, and I needed a couple of minutes at the end of the meeting to discuss the real reason I wanted to see him. I prayed he would make up his mind about the $2,000,000 quickly.

"Rolf," I said, "here are six proposals based on the zero-cost concept I discussed with you over the phone. The death benefit returns the original face amount, plus the premiums, plus what those premiums would have earned had you invested them elsewhere."

Rolf took the proposals from me, and studied them, spending about twenty seconds on each. The fifth proposal would be my recommendation. The premium stream and the interest rate involved best suited his needs. If he selected the fifth proposal, I would have time left to discuss the real reason for my visit. I prayed hard. While Rolf continued to look at the proposals, I placed my hands on my lap and concentrated on steadying them. I have a tendency to tap my fingers nervously, and now would be a rather untimely occasion to indulge in a distracting habit. I turned to look outside and watched as one bird chased another around in the air. Perhaps the pursuer was trying to sell the other insurance.

After two minutes, Rolf looked up. "Proposal number five," he declared.

"That is my recommendation."

"Fine, then, thank you, David."

"Rolf," I said, "I still have eleven more minutes of your time–"

Rolf looked at his watch.

"So you do," he said. I knew Rolf was a man of his word.

"Rolf, I would like to meet with you and your lawyers and accountants. I want to develop a package of insurance for the new partnership – based on this zero-cost plan. Can we arrange an appointment to discuss this?" I asked.

Rolf was the de facto head partner of a packaging company that was undergoing a massive restructuring. I had done insurance for the original partnership years before when they bought out an international company. It was my biggest case – a total of $42,000,000 of insurance. But since then, the company had grown tremendously. Now the insurance need would be around $100,000,000 – and I wanted a shot at the business. The fact that I had done the original insurance would help me – but not as much as I would like. Each of the 10 partners would be bringing in their own agents and the competition would be fierce. But I knew Rolf was the kingpin, whoever had his support would likely win the business. I needed him to agree to an appointment. His eyes turned and he looked me straight in the face, as though he were probing my mind for any weakness. If I flinched, he would say no. It was as simple as that.

I stared back unblinking. Rolf said yes.

Break through to selling megacases

As I drove back home, barely aware of the road and the increasing traffic, I wondered how in the world I had found myself in a position where I was asking a client for an appointment to discuss $100,000,000 worth of insurance. Thirty years earlier I had arrived in Toronto as an immigrant – virtually penniless. And somehow, since then, I had managed to rise to the top of the insurance business. As I thought about it, I realized that the answer was not really a mystery. In fact, the meeting with Rolf was an inevitable milestone on the path that I had chosen and created for myself. Since those first days in Canada, I had dreamed that I would meet people like Rolf, earn their confidence and do business with them. This book is about the strategies I developed to help me realize those dreams.

I have written this book in the hope that others might be able to use some of my strategies to realize their own dreams. The truth is, if I can do it, so can you. I have never felt I was a natural salesperson. When I was a young agent, I would marvel at the ease with which the other new salespeople seemed to sell. If they made it look easy, I made it look difficult. But, because I wasn't a natural, I was forced to develop strategies to help me sell, first small insurance policies, then larger and larger ones, until I eventually broke through to selling megacases – cases where the insurance amount is $10,000,000 or more. In this book, I will show you all of the strategies I used to take my business and sales to the top. And, yes, I will tell you how the case with Rolf turned out – but first, the lean years.

PART II

How to lay the foundation
for taking your business to the top

There was only one possible

way of avoiding my inevitable dismissal

on Monday and that was to make

a sale over the weekend.

I would have to do in two days

what I hadn't been able to do

in two months, otherwise

my plan would be ruined.

CHAPTER 2

Creative survival in the lean years

Y ou'll soon see that I didn't start off my insurance career with a bang. Rather, I struggled and made many mistakes along the way. But I did learn one thing in my first few months in the business – how to survive. In this chapter, I'll tell you the story of how I got into the insurance business and some of my early struggles. I'll show you the methods I used to survive, which I sum up in the phrase 'Creative Survival.' Learning how to survive is not only important in the beginning of someone's career, especially one in the insurance business, but also crucial throughout a career that – like mine – is bound to go through many cycles, some of them difficult. Bouncing back from tough weeks, months, or even tough years, is one of the key ingredients to success.

So, I'll begin this chapter with how I got my start in the insurance business. I'll show you my 4 strategies for creative survival: 1) See yourself today as you want to be tomorrow. 2) Develop a plan and stick to it. 3) Find the courage to open doors and close sales. 4) Hold personal strategy sessions. Then I'll end it with how, many years later, I managed to bounce back from a rather dark period in my life.

Strategy 1: See yourself today as you want to be tomorrow

The traffic cleared and Hans put the pedal to the floor. The half-open passenger window beside me started rattling from the wind and I leaned down to roll it up. I struggled with the stiff handle, finally managing to get the window close to the top, where it stuck, letting the air whistle in at a high pitch.

"Hans," I said, "you have to repair this window."

"I'd love to, David, believe me, but Mr. McDougall won't part with the money – he's a true Scot."

"Hey, watch it, Hans, I'm Scottish."

"Yeah, but *you* can't keep a dollar in your pocket for more than a minute."

"I'm a big spender," I said with a shrug.

Hans laughed, "No offense, but isn't big spending for wealthy people?"

"I believe you've got to see it in your head first, then the money will follow. I see myself as a wealthy man who has a big house, a family, and takes vacations in warm places," I said. "You can't get anywhere in life by settling for what you have today."

"You're never satisfied."

"No, I'm not, and that's why I will be successful."

A big, tail-finned Chevy swerved in front of us and Hans slammed on the breaks, torpedoing me towards the windshield. I braced myself against the dash to avoid head injury as we screeched to a halt. As I slumped back into my seat, Hans sighed, "David, if you were wealthy you'd get yourself a car instead of trusting your life with me."

"I have my eye on a Thunderbird, white with a red interior," I said staunchly.

Strategy 2: Develop a plan and stick to it

Even as a young man growing up in Scotland, I had always dreamed of being wealthy. But from a very early age, I knew that my dream would not become a reality unless I developed workable plans for achieving my goals and stuck to them.

In Scotland I was making ends meet as an interior decorator and part-time tenor, but unfortunately my country was crumbling around me. I saw my dream of becoming wealthy slip away from me as a socialist government came into power and the country's economy began to fail. Although some of my business associates at the time were content to watch their businesses dry up, I developed a plan for turning my life around.

The first step in my plan was obvious – I needed to pull up my stakes and make a new start. I love my family, my homeland, and my heritage, but in 1957, I looked across the ocean to North America and saw a land where the economy was growing and opportunity abounded. I planned to transplant my interior decorating business to Canada.

On March 10, 1957, I arrived in Toronto and knew immediately that I had made the right decision. I was 29 at the time and remember walking up University Avenue, the main business corridor, and seeing cranes and scaffolding, workmen buzzing around. I thought of Scotland with its half-empty buildings and the listless, aimless way people moved about on its streets. Here there was activity, the promise of wealth.

How I got into the paint-selling business

Living in a country where wealth was achievable, was a step in the right direction. But I knew that in order to become wealthy I would have to work for myself. So, my long-term plan was to start my own business. However, I literally had only $40 dollars in my pocket. So my short-term plan was to use my experience to find work in the interior decorating business in order to make ends meet.

In the small living room of the apartment I rented above a laundromat, I began looking up local interior decorating companies in the phone book. The first few numbers I called were no longer in service, but finally I reached somebody at Stan and Associates, Exteriors & Interiors. Unfortunately, the woman who answered the phone told me they were now strictly in the exteriors business and planned to change their name to avoid phone calls like mine.

"The department stores are doing it all," she said, "Everybody has closed down but them. They've got a monarchy."

"Monopoly, you mean," I corrected her.

"Yeah, that's right."

I thanked her for the wonderful news and riffled through the phone book, looking for the numbers of all the department stores. That proved to be a dead end. They were all sufficiently staffed and had a rather large pile of resumés. I was welcome to add mine to the bottom if I wished. But unless they planned on starting at the bottom and had a job for me in the morning, there wasn't much point.

There weren't any opportunities in the interior decorating business, but I still thought that my short-term plan to leverage my experience made sense. I knew about color, finishes, and paints, so I made a list of jobs requiring that knowledge. I came up with painting, working in the office of a paint company, and selling paint. Because my long-term plan was to eventually work for myself, my choice was obvious. Selling paint would give me some control over how much I earned – the more I could sell, the more I would make.

I started looking the next day, and it only took a few calls to find out that a company called McInley & McDougall wanted to expand their sales force. My interview with the tall and thin Mr. McDougall went well, but he turned out to be your stereotypical Scot – tighter than two coats of paint. He offered me a meager base and slim commissions, but I needed the job and it fit into my short-term plan, so I accepted.

Selling paint for McInley & McDougall would be a great opportunity for me – I would be able to cut my teeth in sales – but it would only be a way station on the road to executing my long-term plan – to work for myself.

Strategy 3: Find the courage to open doors and close sales

Simply following your plan doesn't mean things will be easy – you will need the courage to stick to it. Selling turned out to be more difficult than I anticipated. I had to learn to overcome what I call 'hot-doorknob syndrome' – the wave of nausea that washes over you right before knocking on a prospect's door, or right before reaching for the phone to make a cold call. I realized that I wouldn't be able to avoid the nausea – it always came – but I could, with courage, just ignore it. And that's exactly what I did. Once I'd found the courage to approach prospects, I needed to find the courage to try creative approaches when conventional sales techniques failed me. Here's a story where that courage was crucial.

The big pencil

Steven & Sons was a big company and I'd been trying to get their business for a couple of months. Although I hadn't been able to convince the owners to buy any paint from me so far, I was determined to get the sale one way or another.

I used to catch a ride to my sales calls with Hans, the delivery driver for McInley & McDougall. One afternoon, he had a delivery to make to a new store that was just getting ready to open called Peter's Paints. Steven & Sons was just around the corner, so I went with him.

Hans pulled over to the side of the road, just outside Peter's Paints. They were still renovating the store, and the only thing that seemed to be finished was the sign. Outside, on the sidewalk, lay the remnants of the former tenant. From the look of the garbage, I guessed they had been some kind of office stationery or arts supply store. A large, four-foot-long plastic pencil caught my eye, obviously something that had been used in a display.

Hans hopped out of the van and a few moments later I heard him open the back doors. In the side mirror I saw him slide a couple of boxes out and then haul them on a cart through the maze of refuse and into the store.

While he was inside I used the few minutes of silence to meditate on my sale to Steven & Sons. They were partly owned by New England Paints and, by no coincidence, had all their paints supplied by them. Steven & Sons did a lot of work on parking lots, using New England paints, which didn't weather the winters too well. One of our suppliers had the right paint for the job, and that's what I'd been pitching to Steven & Sons. But Johnson, the buyer, wouldn't budge; their relationship with New England Paints was apparently too tight to let another supplier in the door. Because I knew they needed a better paint, I didn't want to give up. I asked Johnson if he would mind if I came by occasionally to see him. He said that would be all right and I dropped by every couple of weeks with coffee and a box of pastries. We got along well, but still he wouldn't buy from me. I needed something to push him over the edge. I racked my brains. I'd told him all the wonders of my paint, I'd promised him a significant discount, I brought him refreshments.... I needed something, but what?

I saw Hans emerge from Peter's Paints, wheeling his cart freely behind him. In a moment he was back in the driver's seat gunning the engine.

"Hold it, Hans," I said, as he was pulling out.

I hopped out of the van, stepped over some garbage and grabbed what I wanted from the heap of junk.

I swung open the back doors and shoved my prize inside, sliding it on top of the boxes of paint.

Back inside the van, Hans looked over at me, his eyes quizzical. "What're you gonna do with that giant pencil?" he asked.

"You'll see," I said, "just take me to Steven & Sons...."

I had a hell of a time negotiating the giant pencil through the front doors of Steven & Sons. Joanne at the front desk laughed at my struggles. "Hi, David," she said with a grin. "I guess your hands were too full for pastries this time?"

"I never come empty handed, Joanne, you know that. They're right here, on the other side of the pencil," I said, nodding at the box dangling from my left pinkie. The string from the pastry box was cutting a deep groove in my flesh.

Joanne eased the box off my finger and led me in to see Johnson, the pencil pivoting wildly on my shoulder.

Johnson looked up from his desk in amazement. "What the heck do you have there, David?"

"I brought this big, giant pencil to help you sign that big, giant order for the parking-lot paint you need," I said, and waited.

Johnson laughed, "Man, you're never gonna give up, are you?"

"Not till you sign for an order."

"All right," Johnson sighed, throwing his hands in the air, "give me the order form. I'll try your paint and see how I like it."

I returned to the van, pencil over my shoulder, grin on my face. "What're you so happy about?" Hans asked.

I told Hans the story and watched him roll his eyeballs. "You're a little crazy, David, but you've got balls, that's for sure. I never thought you'd sell to Steven & Sons in a million years."

"Yeah, Hans, that's the difference, I guess, between you and me.... I knew it all along." I didn't mean it as an insult and Hans didn't take it as one. We liked each other a lot. But we were very different: he was happy where he was, I wasn't. I wanted a lot more out of life, and I was determined to get it.

The thing that I'd needed to close the sale with Steven & Sons wasn't a big, plastic pencil – the pencil could have been any one of a number of props. What I'd needed, and found, was courage, the courage to take a risk on a creative approach.

Revisiting strategy 2: sticking to my plan – short-term pain

Before long, I was faced with another difficult career choice, but because I had a plan to follow I was able to make the right decision.

The sale I made to Steven & Sons impressed McDougall quite a bit. He'd seen many other salespeople attempt to sell them, but nobody had come through. I would make many other valuable sales, and McInley and McDougall, who wanted to make certain I stayed with the company, eventually offered me a partnership. McInley was tighter than McDougall, but the deal was rather sweet. I remember discussing the offer with Hans during one of our deliveries.

"Wow, David, that's amazing. These guys have never offered anyone a partnership before. Hell, I've been working for them longer than anybody, and I've barely gotten a raise."

"Yeah, it's a good deal all right. Too bad I'm not taking it."

Hans hit the brakes, the van stopped suddenly and we were both thrown forward. "Pardon me," he said incredulously. A horn bellowed from behind.

"Hans," I said, "you better start moving, you're holding up traffic." Instead he pulled over to the side of the road.

"You're kidding me, man. Nobody turns down an offer like that."

"I do."

Hans sat in his seat, his jaw hanging loosely. He was a big German man. He'd come over with his family when he was a child, so he didn't have much of an accent, but whenever he got mad or emotional he reverted to his Teutonic roots. "You're a dummkopf," he said. "Why? It don't make any sense."

"I've got a plan, and working for McInley & McDougall isn't in it."

"What's your plan?" he asked.

"Well, my dream is to become wealthy, and my plan for achieving that is to work for myself. Nobody gets rich working for somebody else. I might make a decent living working for McInley & McDougall, but I'm shooting for more than just decent."

"But what are you going to do, exactly?"

"I'm not quite sure. I'm still figuring it out. I'm looking at a few things – the types of careers where you can work for yourself and make a lot of money."

"And what are those?" Hans asked.

"The three that I'm exploring are real estate, securities, and insurance. You can certainly do well in the first two, but there's a problem with them. They're cyclical. When a depression or recession hits, real estate and securities suffer. But insurance is different. You still need insurance when the economy goes through a downturn."

"Yeah, but who's gonna buy insurance then? Nobody's got money when a depression hits." Hans said.

"Truth is, during a depression, the rich get richer and the poor get poorer. And I plan to sell to the rich, anyway."

My plan was a long-term one, and although the decision I made meant I suffered in the short term, I knew it was the right thing to do for my future.

How I got into the insurance business
After a few months of selling paint, I went out and bought a car.

It wasn't the Thunderbird I wanted. It was a large, garish green two-door Buick with a faulty exhaust system, but it would get me around at least. When I phoned to get car insurance, I also inquired about purchasing life insurance. That led to a meeting with an agent from the New York Life Insurance Company, which in turn led to a phone call from Huss Breithaupt, the sales manager. I learned later that Huss was on a recruiting campaign and was scouring the recent insurance applicants for anybody who had anything to do with sales. With 'paint salesman' written on the occupation line of my application I was a sitting duck.

As I had explained to Hans, I was already looking at the insurance business as a possible career move, so the timing of Huss's phone call couldn't have been better. I was impressed with his demeanor over the phone, he was very proper and courteous – not at all the stereotypical salesman. Plus, he explained that my income in the insurance business would be unlimited, and that put me over the edge. He wanted to meet me for lunch the next week, and I asked him if we could make it tomorrow – I didn't want to wait another day to get started on my new life. Huss agreed, and we met for lunch at a restaurant downtown.

When I walked in I saw a trim, dapper fellow seated by himself. I walked over to make sure it was Huss, and introduced myself.

"Cowper," he said, sounding out my name, "that would make you Scottish?"

"And Breithaupt," I replied, "now that's German."

"No, it's Austrian," he replied uppishly.

Back then, the Second World War was still fresh in everyone's mind, and I replied, "Oh, yes, that's right, in 1945 they all became Austrians."

Huss laughed and the ice was broken. We continued to discuss what a career in the insurance business might be like for me. Huss painted a rather pleasant picture of me working for myself, setting my own hours, seeing clients of my choosing. At one point Huss said, "My top salesman at the moment only works two days a week and takes two months off in the summer.... I can only imagine how much he'd make if he worked full time."

"I'll show you. Someday I'll be your number-one salesman and I plan on working a full week."

Huss smiled, "I look forward to it, David."

Huss escorted me back to his office across the street, asked me to write an aptitude test and to call him the following evening for the results.

I called the next night, discovered I had passed and was invited back for another interview. Up till now things had been easy, but a serious snag lay waiting for me in the interview.

The plan begins to pay-off – long-term gain

"David," Huss said, "I need you to write down a list of 100 people."

"People?" I asked confused. "Just a list of people? Anybody?"

"Well, people you know – personally, of course. You know, a list of people you could easily approach to sell insurance to."

I must have gulped visibly.

"You can do that, David," Huss said, "can't you?"

"Sure, absolutely, of course. Who couldn't?"

"Well, you'd be surprised, some people don't get out much, David. I've had some recruits who couldn't give me more than a dozen names."

"I promise you a hundred names, Huss."

"Great, David, bring them in tomorrow and we'll get started."

"Huss, what's the arrangement? As far as base salary goes?" I asked.

"Well, technically, there is no base, David."

"I see," I said, wincing.

"You do get a hundred dollar draw against future earnings, though, and a hundred dollar training allowance every month."

"Thanks," I said, relieved. "And that starts... when?"

"As soon as you bring those hundred names, David."

"Right."

I left his office and went home, meditating on my little problem. One hundred names. I hadn't been in the country long, and knew few people in Toronto on a personal basis. I grabbed a pencil and pad of paper and started with the few people I knew from my paint selling days, then I began listing all the names of everyone I knew who had emigrated to Canada from my hometown Edinburgh. After a half hour or so of scouring my memory I came up with one hundred names – that was the easy part. Yes, I could, in theory ask them to buy insurance, if I knew where I could find them; but thankfully Huss hadn't asked if I knew where they were.

I returned the next day with my list, received my hundred dollar draw and hundred dollar training allowance, then was driven through an intensive six-day training course, and set loose to approach the hundred names on my list.

I remember running into Ivan, one of the six other recruits, in the parking lot shortly after our training. He was a short, round man from Poland who played the concertina. I thought that, as a fellow immigrant, he might share my dilemma.

"Ivan," I asked, "do you really have a hundred people you can ask to buy insurance?"

"Sure, David," he replied, "don't you?"

"Well," I said haltingly, "I'm about to find out, I guess, but surely you don't really know a hundred people in Toronto. Aren't all your friends back home."

"I might have a thick accent, David, but I've lived in Toronto for fifteen years. I play in a large band and know lots of other Polish immigrants. It's a very tight community, David. That's why I got into this business. Nobody I know is selling to the Poles."

"I see," I said and wished him luck as I went looking for my car.

Cold calling

I made my first call to a former customer of mine in the paint business. His name was Tony and I knew he was a father of two. When I rang him, I told him I wasn't selling paint, I was selling insurance now.

"David," he said, "I already have an agent."

"But maybe you'd let me look at your situation to see if there's something missing in your plan."

"The agent is my wife's brother."

"I see," I replied, stumped. I didn't remember any comebacks from our training package that would get around this one.

"David," Tony said, "I wish you luck. But if you ever get back into the paint business let me know, I always liked buying from you."

"Tony," I replied, "I'll never get back into the paint business, but if your brother-in-law ever gets out of the insurance business let me know, I always liked selling to you." He laughed at that and then I moved on through my list.

It didn't take me long to exhaust the few people I knew in Toronto. Most, like Tony, said they already had an agent and wouldn't see me, and the others who agreed to see me wouldn't buy. I then began looking for the people who had emigrated from Scotland. I soon discovered that none of them had moved to Toronto. So cold calling it was. Very cold calling, indeed. I started going through the only other decent list of names I knew – the phone book.

I would call random people up and say, "Hello, I'm David Cowper and I represent the New York Life Insurance Company in your area, and I'd like to come and see you to discuss your plans for protecting your family."

Most of the replies I got were variations on 'buzz off.'

"I don't want no insurance, don't call me again."

"I have an agent already, thank you."

"You're selling insurance! Get lost."

"No thank you, mister."

"My dad's not home."

A perfect sales record

Fortunately Huss gave everybody a little slack for the first couple of weeks as we got our feet wet, but he expected to see some results shortly after that. Unfortunately, after four weeks I still hadn't made a single sale – Huss wasn't the only one concerned about my performance.

By the fifth week, I was making my way through all the Friedmans in the phone book. Discouraged, I decided to take a break for a minute. I turned to Ivan who sat at a desk close to mine.

"Ivan," I said, "how are you making out?"

"Great, David. I've sold thirteen policies so far. I've made it to the top of the sales charts." I glanced over to the chart on the wall

and saw that indeed his name had moved to the top. Quickly my
eye ran down the list of twenty-odd names, finally reaching mine
at the bottom.

"Congratulations, Ivan," I said, "I'm happy for you."

"You're having a little trouble, David, I see," Ivan said solicitously.

"A little," I replied sheepishly.

"What's wrong?" Ivan asked.

"I can't get anybody to buy," I replied.

"I guess that explains it," Ivan said. "Are you making appointments?"

"Some," I said.

The truth was I had trouble even getting an appointment.
I didn't have the personality to really push people over the phone.
Most people didn't want to see an insurance agent, and I couldn't
seem to pry a way into their lives. I had had a couple of
appointments, but couldn't close a sale.

"Well, David, I don't know what to say. Selling comes easy
to me, I guess."

"I guess so." Selling insurance certainly wasn't coming easy for me.
I was determined to stick with it though. I hadn't made the decision to
enter the insurance business lightly, and I had the courage to follow my
plan because I had developed it from sound principles. After all, I'd
given up a partnership in McInley & McDougall for the opportunity to
work for myself and make as much money as I wanted. I believed that
I was selling a good product and that there were lots of people out
there who needed my services. I just needed to hone my skills a little.

While some agents in the office sold six policies one week and
then none the next, I was the only one who could claim perfect
consistency. In the sixth week, I was still shut-out, and Huss was at
the end of his tether. One afternoon I was sitting at my desk with
my hand on the phone and the phone book open on my desk.
I remember seeing an ominous shadow crawl up the gray pages
of the phone book. I sensed Huss's presence, but pretended not
to notice and proceeded to ring a B. Giorgio. I'd called A. Giorgio
just seconds before and discovered that nobody was home.
I was hoping for more luck with one of his probable relatives.

In the middle of dialing, a hand reached over my shoulder and disconnected the call.

"David," Huss said.

"Yes," I replied turning around.

"Set up an appointment for tomorrow afternoon."

"With who?" I asked.

"One of your prospects."

"I'm working on that very thing right now, actually. Mr. B. Giorgio was expecting me to return his call just a few moments ago."

"Great, set up something with Mr. B. Giorgio for tomorrow – for you and me."

"The two of us?" I replied.

"Exactly," Huss said as he turned and left.

I looked over at Ivan who shot me a concerned look. "He wants to do fieldwork with you, David."

"Oh, that's good, I guess," I replied.

"Last guy he did fieldwork with was Simpson."

"Yeah, where is Simpson?" I asked. Simpson had been one of the other recruits along with Ivan and me. Simpson hadn't sold much, in fact, I think he only sold two policies, both of which had recently lapsed.

"He's gone, David," Ivan said.

"Gone?"

"Terminated. Two days ago."

"Oh, I see," I replied, turning around to call Mr. B. Giorgio.

The next morning at the office Huss came by my desk and asked what time the appointment was for.

"Noon," I replied.

"So we should leave here...."

"Eleven-thirty will be plenty of time," I replied.

Fieldwork fiasco

At eleven-thirty I saw Huss open his office door and come down the hall. He was always fastidiously attired, but today there was an air of sartorial perfection about him. A fussy man myself, I admired Huss's attention to detail, his cufflinks newly polished, his handkerchief puffed out, and his wing-tips gleaming.

"Ready, David?"

"Aye, aye, captain."

Two dapper men, we marched out into the parking lot and stepped into my battered, garish-green Buick. My passenger seat was broken and to prop it up I used an unopened soup can, which worked quite well. "This is your car, David?" Huss inquired with a tinge of condescension as he settled into his seat, which must have been a little uncomfortable. Fortunately, Huss couldn't see that the only thing holding his seat up was the soup can.

"A little battered, but trusty. I plan on trading up soon."

"After the sales start coming in, I suspect," Huss replied.

"Indeed."

I turned over the engine, it coughed and sputtered, coming to life haltingly. With a few hearty stomps on the gas pedal, the engine was humming relatively smoothly. I backed out and we were on our way.

A little while later Huss asked where the appointment was.

"On the Danforth," I replied. "Not too much further." Unfortunately Mr. B. Giorgio hadn't actually been home last night. In fact, none of the Giorgios had been home. Nor the Giornos, or the Giottos. And Ms. Giovetti didn't speak much English. So I hadn't actually been able to get an appointment at all. Instead, I was planning on taking Huss to a hardware store I had shopped at once. I was hoping the manager would be in.

At that moment, I noticed a faint whiff of exhaust fumes. I was well aware of Huss's keen sense of smell. He always wore fine cologne himself and complained whenever he encountered the slightest bad odor. There was a distinct pungency about the fumes that were now filling the car, and I knew Huss wouldn't appreciate them.

"David, I think something is wrong with your car." He said, his hand over his nose.

"It'll pass," I said, hoping.

The fumes thickened, and I peered over at Huss who started to turn a shade of green.

"David, please, your car is making me sick. How can you drive with the smell?"

"The first cash I get my hands on I'll use for repairs, I promise."
I felt bad for Huss, having to endure the ride in my Buick. I didn't
enjoy it myself, but at least I'd gotten used to it.

Suddenly Huss yelled, "Stop the car, stop the car!"

I turned and looked out the windshield and saw the rear
of a truck double-parked on the road. I slammed on the break.
Unfortunately, the jolt was too much for the soup can, the seat
back gave way and Huss was thrown heavily on his back.

"My God, you've broken my seat!" I cried.

"Pull the car over to the curb," Huss hissed through
clenched teeth, holding his ribs. I did so and then leaned over
to help him up. He shoved my hands aside, heaved open the
door and jumped out.

I watched nervously as he hailed a cab, never looking back.

Maybe I got lucky – Huss may have been more upset to know
that there never was an appointment. As it was, exasperated as he
might be, he was still under the impression that I did have a
prospect to see. I sat in the car for a few minutes, collecting my
thoughts, and trying to gather the courage to get on with the
day. Certainly I wasn't going back to the office.

I did go to the hardware store only to discover that the
manager was not in. For the rest of the afternoon, I tried other
stores up and down the street, but to no avail.

For the next few days, I laid low at the office, trying to avoid
Huss. I still didn't have a sale and was getting increasingly
concerned about my future in the business. It was not through
lack of trying. I was calling people everyday, just getting nowhere.
Unfortunately, calling people at random is rarely fruitful, but in
my first few months in the business, I didn't have much choice.

The following week, Huss was away on vacation and Jim, his
much tougher assistant, was left in charge. On Monday, Jim came
by to hand out prospect cards to the recruits. Everyone but me
seemed eager to get their hands on them. When Jim offered me
my stack of cards, I told him he could give them to someone else.

"What?" he said, standing there dumbfounded.

"Where did they come from?" I asked.

"From a former agent," he replied.

"Who's no longer here."

"Yeah, that's right, who's no longer here," he said with some annoyance.

"Who's no longer here because he couldn't sell the names on those very cards," I added.

"Listen, David," Jim said, nodding in the direction of the sales chart where my name was firmly ensconced at the bottom, "I think you should take what you can get."

"Jim, those people might as well be dead. Give me some live ones and I'll be all over them."

Jim tossed the cards to Peter, one of my cohorts. Jim turned to leave. "By the way, Jim," I said, "those were Simpson's, weren't they."

Jim snorted and left.

I turned to Peter. "You might as well throw them out," I said.

Under the gun

As the week progressed I was still without a sale and growing more nervous by the minute. The draw and the training allowance were due next week. If you made it through to a draw week you were probably okay for a little while longer, but if you were due for a termination, you were about to find out. Unfortunately for me, Huss was away. I felt, at least, that Huss still retained a modicum of faith in my abilities and that was why I hadn't been terminated yet. Jim, on the other hand, had his gun trained on me. On Friday I had been away all morning on cold calls, and arrived late. I ran into Ivan as I got off the elevator. His eyes were downcast and he was carrying a couple of bags full of stuff.

"Going away for the weekend, Ivan?" I asked.

"No, I've been terminated. Jim just let me go."

"Terminated!" I cried. "But you were doing so well. What about all those policies you placed?"

"Everyone has canceled their insurance. All my policies have lapsed, David."

"I'm so sorry, Ivan."

"I'm sorry for you too, David."

"Me?" I said.

"When you go in, you'll be terminated too."

"Oh," I said, a shudder running through me.

"See ya," Ivan said as he stepped past me to get on the elevator.

I turned and went back into the elevator with Ivan. "Well," I said, "what's the point of going in then?" I rode down with Ivan and we parted outside the building. It was a sad moment. I watched him trundle off, his gait slow and heavy. I felt a heavy sorrow. I had gotten along well with Ivan and truly wished him success. But I was also sad for another person – me. I couldn't imagine my insurance career coming to an end. It didn't make any sense to me. I had such big plans for myself in insurance. Technically it wasn't over yet; I had avoided termination for another couple of days at least. But there was only one possible way of avoiding my inevitable dismissal on Monday and that was to make a sale over the weekend. I would have to do in two days what I hadn't been able to do in two months, otherwise my plan would be ruined.

Strategy 4: Hold personal strategy sessions

I went home Friday night, made a quick meal for myself and then sat down in my reading chair. It was time to strategize. I relaxed, and began to clear my mind and body of worry. I took a few deep breaths, easing all the knots and tight spots in my body. Then I purged all negative thoughts from my mind, and focused only positive energy on the fact that I would sell a policy to somebody this weekend.

This type of strategy session, the fourth thing you need for creative survival, is something that I would continue to do throughout my career, on a regular basis and certainly on every major case I would work on. I've seen too many agents unable to relax and focus properly under stress. But the reality is that a relaxed and open mind is the only way out of a high-pressure situation.

So, sitting there in my reading chair on Friday night I started to think clearly about how I was going to pursue a sale. So far I had tried the phone book which had proved fruitless, and door knocking which had been equally unsuccessful. As a recent immigrant with few connections, those were my only two choices. At least I had narrowed it down. One of those routes would be the way to my sale. But which one? I could do a little of both, but that idea didn't appeal to me. I wanted a more focused approach. I didn't want to spread my energies too thin. I decided to commit myself to one method all weekend. I could start calling people right now over the phone and not stop until I got a sale, or I could hit the pavement and keep walking until I got a sale. I chose to take advantage of my pretty face....

I rose at 5:30 the next morning, walked down to the coffee shop for a coffee and a pastry and then I was off and running. Since it was the weekend I knew I had my work cut out for me. Most people would be busy shopping or at home relaxing, and very few of them would be in the mood for a salesman. My strategy was to catch somebody who was working on Saturday and taking a break. Within a few moments I saw my first target – a window washer sitting on a park bench next to his squeegee and bucket sipping coffee.

"Excuse me, sir, would you mind if I took a break from my work with you?"

He shrugged his shoulders, so I sat down beside him. "You're a window washer, I gather."

"No guff," he said.

There was silence while I waited for him to return the question. None came, so I offered the information up myself. "I sell peace of mind," I said.

"You one of them bible thumpers," he replied.

"No, no, not at all. I represent the New York Life Insurance Company for this area."

"Insurance?" he said, shuffling a few inches away from me.

"Yes," I answered, "do you have a family?"

"I got a dog," he said. "And I don't care to leave him no money."

"Well–"

He got up and left. Undeterred, I marched on, looking for

my sale. Unfortunately, the day continued as it had begun. And so did Sunday morning.

My first sale

It was close to 5 o'clock on Sunday afternoon and still no sale. I was coming down to the wire, but I was not going to give up. Although I had moments of doubt, I still knew in my heart that I would make a sale this weekend. And there it was, down the street, probably my last hope – a man putting his ladder in the back of his truck. I quickened my pace.

When I got there, he was throwing his tool kit on the passenger seat.

"Excuse me, sir," I said.

"Yeah," he said, a little taken aback. He was dressed in torn jeans, a filthy white sleeveless shirt, and old workman boots. He looked exhausted.

"How are you doing today?"

"I'm tired," he said in a thick Portuguese accent.

"Are you a roofer?" I asked.

"Why, you need roof work?"

"Someday, I hope to, but not today. That's not why I stopped you."

"Well, I gotta get home, now. My wife and kids are waiting for me."

"Before you go, can I ask you one question?"

"Yeah, okay."

"You have to be in pretty good condition to do roof work?" I asked.

He looked at me and saw that I didn't possess a body fit enough for his kind of work. "You want to do roofs?" he asked, smiling.

"No, I'd just like to ask you what you would do if you slipped off the roof one day?"

"I'd go to the hospital," he replied.

I nodded. "Let me put it this way – you make your money by going up on people's roofs. And if you can't make it up there for a month, or two months, you wouldn't be making any money, right?"

"Yeah," he said.

"So, how would you take care of your wife and kids if you fell?" I asked.

He thought about it for a moment. "I dunno," he said. "You got an answer, or what?"

"In fact, I do. I have a plan especially designed for roofers like you. My plan says that if you fall and get injured and you can't work, we'll pay you the money you'd make if you could work."

"You pay me to fix the roof even if I can't fix the roof?" he asked.

"That's what I said."

"How much does this thing cost?"

On Monday morning I walked into the New York Life Insurance offices with my first sale. I was thrilled. It was one of the happiest days of my life. It wasn't a life policy, but it was good enough, an accident and sickness policy. I knew Huss would be in his office with my termination papers on his desk and I wanted to preempt him.

I marched down the hall, and barged into his office, grinning madly. I tossed the signed application on his desk.

"My first sale, Huss. I'm so excited. It's the beginning of a roll for me. I can feel it in my bones. I know I made a slow start, but I've found my footing, your patience is going to start paying off."

Huss looked back at me, a confused look on his face. I kept grinning. Slowly, a smile began to creep across his face. I saw him secretly slide an envelope under a pile of papers. I knew that envelope had my name on it.

"David," he said, "I knew you'd pull through. I knew it all along."

Later in the day, I received a written note from him that read, "Congratulations, David, now try for some life."

Bouncing back

I did eventually write some life insurance, but during my first few months in the business I continued to struggle to survive. I was living from sale to sale, eating up my draw almost as soon as I got it each month. I believed in the logic and long-term value of my plan, but I was sorely tempted when a paint company, a rival of my former employer, McInley & McDougall, offered me a position as vice-president of their company. The salary they dangled in front of my nose dwarfed the offer McInley & McDougall had made to me months earlier. Again, everyone thought I was foolish to turn it down, but that's exactly what I did. It simply wasn't part of my plan. Even though I was having a hard time in the insurance business, I saw a bright future for myself in it. I must have seemed crazy at the time, but I was the only one who knew that accepting an offer for vice-president would mean denying my potential.

Thankfully, as the months wore on, I began to sell more regularly. When merely surviving seemed less of an issue, I began to devote more time to improving my selling methods. I soon developed a set of strategies that had tremendous side effects – my monthly sales results started to climb at a fantastic rate. I'll be exploring those strategies in the coming chapters, but for now, it's enough to tell you that I soon found my footing in the business. I became the provincial leader for New York Life in 1959, my first calendar year in the business. And then, three years later in 1962, I qualified for the Million Dollar Round Table. From there, I continued to strive upwards, always reaching for bigger and better markets. In 1977 I joined the elite in the insurance business as a founding member of the Top of the Table.

My first few years in the business showed me that I could make immense strides in a short period of time. What I proved to myself was that you can take stock of your life at any time, and, if you're unhappy with it, you can go out and change it. I saw that, if you construct a logical plan and stick to it, you don't have to wait decades to see results. But before I go any further in this book I want to talk about how confidence in your plan can help you bounce back from trouble or disaster later in your career.

Life is not a straight line, rather it moves in cycles. I have seen many people, some of them close friends, make it big then lose it all. Some of those people wither away after losing it, some of them bounce back. It's the people that can, as they say in boxing, 'come up off the canvas,' that I truly admire. Whenever I hear of salespeople who have had an exceptional year, the question that comes to mind is, "Great, but can you do it again?" In life, you are often asked to do it again. I know I was.

My tough years

In the early '80s, my life suddenly became very difficult. I suffered a plague of personal and business disasters that escalated in severity. I could devote a few chapters to what happened to me during that time, but I won't. I don't like to dwell on negative things, but I do want to briefly mention a few of the many obstacles I had to overcome as a way of showing you that, even after years of success, you sometimes have to go back into the ring again.

In 1982, I left the insurance industry to embark on a promising career as president of a trust company. Shortly after making the career change, the chairman and major shareholder of the trust company became embroiled in one of the province's most notorious lawsuits, tainting the reputations of all the companies he owned, including the one I was president of. The trust company was seized by the government and I was out of a job. Then, when I went to get my life insurance license back in January of 1983, I was refused. Although I certainly had nothing to do with the lawsuits, my reputation had been damaged by association. In fact, the Department of Insurance wanted me to admit to doing something wrong. I absolutely refused. Only after I wrote them a letter saying, "I promise not to do in the future what it was that I had not done in the past," did they return my insurance license. But by then it was August and I was financially drained, with thousands of dollars in outstanding legal fees. After a quarter of a century of success I had been in a position to retire, but now found myself having to fight to survive again. Many in the insurance industry had called me a legend in the business, and now I was going to have to find out just how good I really was.

I remember thinking back to my early years in the business. I dredged up all the methods I had used to survive back then in order to get through the coming months. I focused on seeing myself as I wanted to be in the future, I made my plan and stuck to it, and with courage and many, many personal strategy sessions, I forged on. By following those simple strategies that I had learned thirty years earlier, I turned my fortunes around. Fortunately, insurance is a business where, because there is always a need for your services, you can orchestrate your own recovery. Remember, the real estate and securities industries can't boast the same. By the end of the year, my commissions were close to what they had been at my peak back in the '70s.

A couple of years later, I wrote one of my biggest cases, the commission on which was a fair portion of my income that year. But as Shakespeare wrote once, "Sorrows never come as single spies, they come in battalions." Before a year was out, the policyholder lapsed the policy. It was devastating. This lapse took me below my bonus schedule with the insurer. I not only had to pay back all the advanced commission on the case, I had to pay back a 20% bonus that had been paid on all of my business with that insurer. Again I found myself fighting back for the rest of the year. And then, just as things got rolling, another change hit me.

Up off the canvas

In 1988, I discovered I had cancer. I endured six and a half weeks of radiation therapy, and because I couldn't afford to take time off from selling insurance, I had to schedule the therapy for early in the morning so I could still go to the office for the rest of the day. I never actually saw anyone in person because, as a way of mapping out the therapy the doctors marked my face with crayon lines and, with those lines and the radiation burns that I developed on my face, I was afraid of spooking my clients and prospects. Unfortunately, the doctors were also predicting I would temporarily lose my voice because of the radiation. So, I decided to prospect during the short time I had left until I lost my voice. I actually ended up calling so many prospects and clients that I did lose my voice for a while, but from too much talking, not from the radiation. I lined up all my appointments for after my therapy. As it happened, I had lots of cases to work on after the doctors were finished with me. By the way, the cancer was many years ago, and I'm fine now. I never doubted that I would recover. Whenever I find obstacles in my way, I fall back on my creative survival strategies. Even though I had cancer, and the treatments were torturous, I saw myself as being healthy and successful in the future. I was confident about my success, because I had a plan and I stuck to it. It took courage and a number of personal strategy sessions during the course of my treatment, but afterwards, I found myself more successful than before.

George Bernard Shaw captured the essence of bouncing back when he said:

> *People are always blaming their circumstances*
> *for what they are. I don't believe in circumstances.*
> *The people who get on in this world are the people*
> *who get up and look for the circumstances they want,*
> *and if they can't find them, make them.*

Four strategies for creative survival

1) SEE YOURSELF TODAY AS YOU WANT TO BE TOMORROW.

2) DEVELOP A PLAN AND STICK TO IT.

3) FIND THE COURAGE TO OPEN DOORS AND CLOSE SALES.

4) HOLD PERSONAL STRATEGY SESSIONS.

We don't earn a living, we learn a living.

CHAPTER 3

The knowledge breakthrough

After learning how to survive I decided to really put my head down and make a success out of myself in the insurance business. I realized I could not do this without knowledge. In this chapter, I will show you 3 strategies for using knowledge to close cases: 1) Know your products. 2) Make information your own. 3) Know your industry.

Let me start by telling you a story about how I used my first strategy in a difficult case.

Strategy 1: Know your products

The young doctor turned to face me, putting down his charts and sliding his pen back into his pocket. "I don't know why you're here talking to me about this," he said.

I looked around the small office that this anesthetist used when he was between surgeries. The walls were drab and unadorned. It was cheerless and stark under harsh white fluorescent lighting.

"As an insurance agent," I said, "if I didn't make an effort to come and speak to you, wouldn't I be remiss in my professional duties?"

"How do you mean?"

"Well, I'm not just here to sell you insurance so that I can make my commission and pay the rent. I have a professional obligation to ensure that your family is provided for in the event that you pass on. Our concern here should be for your wife and your two children, don't you think?"

"Hmmmm, sure," he replied, after a brief pause.

"Well, as I can show you, if you were to purchase whole life insurance, costing you, say $20,000 per year – a small percentage of your actual salary – you would then have a policy in effect worth $1,000,000 to your wife and children upon your death. Think about how that might offset some of the pain and trouble they are bound to experience."

"Well, some other agent was in here a few weeks ago trying to sell me one of those whole life policies," Dr. Levray began. "He was telling me that some portion of my annual premium would build up inside the policy as a cash value. The longer I pay, the closer my total cash value gets to the $1 million face amount. If I live a very long time, all you'll really be doing is giving me my money back, because when I die your company will give my wife the $1 million, but it's going to keep the cash value. To me that's a rip-off."

Dr. Levray certainly knew a lot about insurance, but I thought I had the answer to his concern. I had recently read a brochure that had come across my desk which advertised a new option, known as the fifth-dividend option, which would apply in Dr. Levray's case because the type of plan we were discussing was a participating policy. In such a policy the premium is based on the insurance company making a conservative return on its investment, and if the insurance company's actual returns are higher, a dividend will be issued to the policyholder. Traditionally, a policyholder could choose between four dividend options: 1) take the dividend as cash; 2) use it to purchase more insurance; 3) use it to reduce the premium; or 4) leave it inside the policy and earn interest on it. It was apparent that Dr. Levray knew that none of these options dealt with his concern. However, this new fifth-dividend option met his objection head on – it allowed policyholders to receive the face amount of the policy plus the cash value upon their deaths. I could have told him about this new option now, but I wanted to wait until I was certain that introducing this solution would close the sale.

"Dr. Levray," I said, "you are an astute young man. I can see how you came to hold your current position. In fact, I agree completely with your objection. It doesn't seem fair at all that you should have to forfeit your cash value when you die.

"So please allow me to take a crack at overcoming your objection. Could we meet again next Tuesday? Perhaps at the same time?"

He paused for a moment, thinking it over.

"Don't forget," I added, "you agreed that you did want to protect Mrs. Levray and the children. That hasn't changed. Let me try to solve this problem for you."

"Okay, okay," he said, with a slight smirk. I got the impression he thought I couldn't do it.

Solving the stubborn doctor

Exactly one week later I found myself back in that tiny room sitting across from Dr. Levray again. He wore a white smock and green surgical garb underneath. The desk between us was clean and almost empty of paper. He was obviously a methodical and detail-oriented man.

"So, Doctor," I began, "I think I understand what your objection to purchasing this whole life insurance plan was, but just to make sure I have it right, why don't you tell it to me again in your own words?"

He smiled and sat up straighter in his wooden swivel chair. "When I die you guys keep the cash value."

"Is that the only thing holding you back?" I asked.

"Yes," he replied.

"Okay," I smiled, "if, hypothetically speaking, I could give you a policy that would address that concern, would you be prepared to write me a check?"

"Sure I would," he grinned smugly, letting his pride get the better of him. He thought he had me on a technicality, a loophole he had found. He was sure he wouldn't need to reach for his checkbook because he had uncovered the 'scam' behind life insurance.

"Well then, congratulations," I said, "you've uncovered an important problem with the way our policies are structured and have been instrumental in rectifying the problem."

His eyebrows went up. A curious look slid across his face.

"As a result of your objection I went back to the life insurance company and together we've had to come up with an entirely new option, the fifth-dividend option. It's a special offer, just to address your concern. On your death they are willing to offer you the $1,000,000 face amount of your policy, plus whatever cash value has accrued."

Then, passing him the pen, I said, "Sign here, please."

Learning a living

Whether he realized it or not, Dr. Levray signed that application because I knew my products. I like to say that in this industry we don't earn a living, we learn a living. Knowing my products inside-out and keeping abreast of the most recent developments clinched deals I would have otherwise lost. I don't regard the brochures that flood my office, the ones sent out by all the different life companies, as junk mail. The flyer I remembered reading, the one explaining the new fifth-dividend option, had been generally circulated and had passed across every agent's desk. But as far as I know, I was the first agent in our branch to change the information in that brochure into commissions.

Strategy 2: Make information your own

The reason I am able to change information into commissions is because I make information my own. For me, this means scouring everything that comes across my desk for its hidden meaning. I always ask myself what any piece of information means to my business. Immediately after reading the brochure describing the fifth-dividend option, I tried to figure out how I could use it in a case and realized that this option was the perfect answer to the objection that the death benefit does not return the cash value. As you saw, this turned out to be Dr. Levray's primary objection, and because I had made the information my own, I was able to close the case.

Strategy 3: Know your industry

This strategy is best illustrated by a case that would eventually grow to become the $100,000,000 case, the one I discussed with Rolf in the limo in Chapter 1.

The beginning of the $100,000,000 case

It all started with a speech I gave at a Toronto financial conference in 1979. For weeks prior to taking the stage in the elegant main ballroom of the Royal York Hotel I had been nervous and excited. Just a few months before I had come up with a brand new insurance concept which I felt sure would open new vistas for me. I just had no idea how far those horizons would reach when I took my place behind the rostrum and introduced myself and my topic, the Substitute Creditor, which I will discuss in more detail in chapter 11.

I spoke excitedly for twenty minutes to the captive audience of financial experts, lawyers, executives, and journalists seated at the tables crowded in front of me. Several times I stopped to sip from my water glass and noticed that the people in the front rows seemed to be scribbling frantically. I remember hoping that they were copying down the points I had labored so hard to come up with and not doodling or writing notes to colleagues back at the office. Luckily all my apprehensions were washed away by a sizable wave of applause as I finally closed my remarks and stepped away from the rostrum. I was relieved and more convinced than ever of the value of the Substitute Creditor and my place in the financial community.

As I walked off the right side of the stage, the organizer of the conference stopped me to shake my hand and thank me for speaking. As we stood there talking, a short, stocky man in a black suit approached me and held out his hand.

"My name's Keith Renberg," he said. "I enjoyed your speech and wanted to introduce myself. I think I may have a proposal you'd be interested in hearing."

I said hello and then waited to hear what he had to say. I'd heard of Renberg through my network of financial contacts but we'd never met. I knew he represented a number of companies in the city and that was enough to catch my attention. However, I make a habit of keeping my mouth closed when I'm short on information in a discussion. It's the only way to acquire knowledge from other people; after all, you can't listen if your lips are moving and you can't learn if you can't hear someone else's ideas.

After a brief pause, Renberg said, "I like the idea of the Substitute Creditor. I'm involved in a deal where that type of solution might be the way to go."

My interest was piqued. If they were going to use the idea of the Substitute Creditor I wanted to be involved.

"Can you tell me more about your deal?" I asked.

"We need someone who can underpin credit lines and your Substitute Creditor idea seems to accomplish that." I nodded. "We have a group of 12 executives borrowing $42 million to purchase the packaging company that employs them," he continued.

"Well, I very much doubt there's 12 people all borrowing from the bank," I replied.

Slightly taken back, he looked at me curiously, and said, "Of course there are. There's 12 of them and they each need to put up collateral to raise the total amount."

"I'm sure they do," I said. "But I suspect only two or three of them are negotiating with the bank. They may all need to sign for the loan, but my experience in deals of this size is that a few of the partners act as principals. There is always a core group of key people and usually one or two of them are the real valuable commodities. Although all 12 need to be insured, those two or three are the people that really need special attention. That's where the bulk of your risk is Mr. Renberg."

"Er, you have a point there," he said, considering this new information for a moment. "Perhaps I should get you involved. There are other agents trying to get the case, but it sounds like you have the knowledge required for the complexity and size of this deal. Rolf is the head partner. You will be dealing with his lawyer, Mr. Richards. I'll have him call you."

The suicide clause
Three days later I stepped through Mr. Richard's heavy mahogany

door and into his sparsely furnished office. It was lined with an expanse of deep green carpet. There were no paintings on the wall. Two leather chairs sat empty in front of his solid desk. Mr. Richards sat with his back to the corner windows which overlooked the busy intersection of King and Bay Streets in the heart of Toronto's financial district.

He rose slowly and greeted me in a proper English accent, then folded his thin frame back into his chair.

Once I was seated he carefully placed an ominously large contract on the desk in front of me. It was 90 pages long. "This is the contract my clients are entering into, Mr. Cowper," he said. "I would like you to review it and give me your impressions and thoughts."

Hefting the inch of papers in my hand, I said, "When will we meet again to go over this? I'm anxious to move forward with the case."

"Oh, I'm afraid I can't allow you to leave this office with the document, Mr. Cowper," he said, without blinking. "My clients insist on the utmost confidentiality."

My breath got trapped in my throat and I'm sure my eyes must have bulged. I could understand his clients' need for secrecy but I have always staked my professional reputation on the fact that I never reveal such information. No argument worked with him though. After a couple of tiresome minutes of discussion I gave in and began to go through the document, searching for the paragraphs dealing with the insurance.

While I leafed through it, Mr. Richards sat across from me at his desk, reading papers and making notes. Finally, on page 56 I found what I was looking for, and I began to read much more carefully. It was very thorough. But as I read to the end of the section I realized there was something he had forgotten.

When I cleared my throat he looked up at me over his glasses. "Congratulations on a superb job," I said. "It is very well written and almost totally complete. But it is missing one crucial item."

"And what would that be, Mr. Cowper?" he asked, stiffly.

"It doesn't deal with the suicide clause...."

"What do you mean, suicide clause?"

"Every new policy written in this country is legally required to contain a two-year suicide clause," I explained. "In a deal of the size we are talking about, with so much at risk, I think you should be wary of the consequences of a suicide. If one of the partners were to commit suicide within the two-year waiver, the insurance company would not pay out the death benefit."

His expression did not change, but he did pause for a moment before speaking, a sign that his apple cart had been upset. "Sir, I have drafted hundreds of these buy-sell agreements and have worked with over a dozen insurance agents in the past, but you are the first to tell me about the suicide clause."

I believe it was on that basis that I received the go-ahead to do the deal. As his partner had said, they were looking for somebody with the experience and confidence to complete a case of this size. From my brief encounter with him I realized the players in this deal were consummate professionals whose sole interests were financial success. He must have seen that I knew my business and had the ability to work with the minutiae and detail that such a case would entail. I had been able to find the weak spot, the Achilles Heel, in the contract where others had not, even though they should have been armed with the same knowledge as myself. I think I convinced him on that day that I had the financial and legal well-being of his clients at heart rather than my own gain.

Knowledge gives you confidence

The deal was enormously complex, and I worked as part of a team of lawyers and financial advisors. Rolf, the head partner, was pushing hard for a quick resolution, and we were all under extreme pressure to deliver the goods on an almost impossible schedule, while making absolutely sure we didn't make a mistake that could cost these 12 men their careers, homes and families. To develop the right insurance proposal, I had to call on all of my knowledge of how the insurance industry works. I looked at dozens of insurance companies and explored a myriad of solutions. Because I know the industry, I was confident I had thoroughly examined all possible options, and would be presenting the right proposal. I was able to speak with authority to the entire cast of characters involved – from the client to their accountants, lawyers, and chief financial officers, to the home-office underwriters and actuaries, and, finally, to the reinsurers. As the following scene will show, the confidence I gained from knowing my industry closed the deal.

The confident close

After I put the finishing touches on my proposal, I passed it along to the partners for approval. They reviewed it with their advisors, and that's when things almost fell apart.

Mr. Lerouz, Rolf's accountant, called me into his office on a Thursday. After I sat down, he said, "I've reviewed your proposal, but because I have to look out for my clients' best interests, I need to be convinced that we're getting the absolute lowest rates possible. The amounts involved are so large that a difference of even a fraction of a percent could generate significant savings. I would like you to come back with some competing quotes."

I remained calm, even though I could envision the legwork I would have to do if he got his way. "Mr. Lerouz," I said, "I assure you that I have surveyed all of the products and prices available to us and have presented you with the most balanced package for your needs. For three reasons, I can guarantee there wouldn't be a meaningful difference between the rates you have in front of you now, and any new rates I could possibly get.

"First, I've placed the insurance with a company willing to give the partners the most charitable medical rating possible and so their premiums are already much lower than they would be anywhere else. If the partners were rated medically higher by a company with lower basic rates, we would end up spending more. Asking me to go chasing my tail around the industry could put us in a far worse position.

"Second, if the company I have already suggested gets wind of our efforts to undercut them, they may withdraw their initial offer altogether.

"Third, you've told me you want to see competitive quotes because you are working for your clients' best interests and trying to save them money. That's admirable, but the cost to Rolf of having you repackage this deal over the weekend would dwarf any difference in rates that I might be able to get you. The bottom line, Mr. Lerouz, is that I think that what we've given you is a very balanced package, thoughtfully underwritten, and I would strongly advise against any changes at this point."

I endured a nervous moment of silence while he thought over what I had said. Then finally, with a laugh, he said, "True enough, you've convinced me I have every reason to trust your recommendation."

With Lerouz's approval the case was closed, and the buy-out went ahead smoothly. I owe the close of this $42,000,000 case to the knowledge strategies I have shown you in this chapter. Because I knew my products, specifically the suicide clause, and because I made that information my own, I was chosen to do the deal, and it was my thorough knowledge of the industry that took me the rest of the way.

In chapter 9, I'll show you how I was able to return to this case and take it to the next level – $100,000,000.

Three strategies for using knowledge to close cases

1) KNOW YOUR PRODUCTS.

2) MAKE INFORMATION YOUR OWN.

3) KNOW YOUR INDUSTRY.

"... You charge back into

the smoke and, coughing and choking,

you quickly realize that you can save

only four people.

Tell me, sir, who would you save,

four of your creditors or your

wife and three children?"

CHAPTER 4

The power of passion

As we saw in the last chapter, knowledge is crucial to making sales. But sometimes knowledge is not enough – you also need passion. Early in my career I developed a passion for selling insurance, a passion that runs deep, even to this day. In order to break through to megacase selling, you need to really believe in the power of your product. In this chapter, I'll show you 5 strategies for using passion to close challenging cases: 1) Find your own passion. 2) Have passion for the promise. 3) Be passionate about your products. 4) Be passionate about your business. 5) Use your passion to close cases.

Strategy 1: Find your own passion

Most agents who have such a genuine belief in the power of their product have had what I call a defining moment in which they realized the true benefit of their product to the client. Let me tell you about mine, and later I'll show you how it helped me to close a case I otherwise would never have completed.

Sacrifice
One evening, soon after I started in the life insurance business, I found myself sitting across a wooden kitchen table from a

blue-shirted Italian man and his aproned wife. The dinner dishes sat in a rubber tray on the counter, drying. Heavy smells of cooked meat and sauces lingered in the air and my stomach grumbled with displeasure. In my rush to come and see this couple I'd dodged my own supper.

The old man had bright eyes and watched me intently, waiting to hear what I had to say. He worked on the line at a large factory in the east end, spending hours every day drilling holes, while his wife struggled at home, cleaning the house and looking after their three children. What I told him, as gently and as clearly as I could, was that I could guarantee his family would be well taken care of after his death if he could put aside just a small sum every year.

He looked at his wife. She looked down and then turned to face him.

"John, John," she said, "the kids they need clothes now, we need a new refrigerator and a new couch. How can we spend that money?"

John turned to face me. "It's hard," he said. "We don't have a lot, and what you're asking for is, I think, too much." He raised his hands in a genuine gesture of helplessness.

I smiled warmly. "Mr. Napoli, you can still afford those things. I'm not asking you to sacrifice your children's clothes or things for the house. But money you invest now, while you are working and healthy, can take care of your family should you lose your health or die."

He turned to his wife and they spoke briefly and quickly in Italian.

Facing me again he said, "Mr. Cowper, I thank you for coming to our house tonight. There is a lot of value in what you've said. But my wife and I must really think about what you're asking. It's a big decision, you understand, and there's so many other things we need to consider. Please, give us a week to think about it and then call me again."

I left their small bungalow that night thinking I had a good chance of making the sale. At that time I was close to selling $5,000 worth of premiums for the month and was really starting to get somewhere.

But a week later, when I called to find out the result of their discussions, he told me they had no choice but to put their money elsewhere for now. He agreed with me that his family needed to be taken care of, but they couldn't afford it. I've never been a high-pressure type of salesman. If I've said all I can say and somebody tells me they aren't interested, they aren't interested. So I thanked him and told him to call me if his situation changed.

The $50,000 mistake

Several years later I was driving through that neighborhood again and saw a For Sale sign on the lawn of that same brick bungalow. I wondered if they had decided to trade up now that the kids were older. Perhaps they needed more room. Perhaps his job had been going well. After all that time, perhaps they would be more receptive to the idea of planning for the future.

I rang the doorbell and the man's wife, Maria, answered the door. She was a little bit more gray, seemed a little more stooped and her clothes and the house were dark. I smiled, said hello, and asked her if she remembered me from my previous visit. "Si," she said and looked down at her slippers. Motioning me inside the house, she led me wordlessly to the kitchen. I expected her to call for her husband to join us. Instead she took me to the large green refrigerator in the corner. We stood silently for a second. I was confused until she said, firmly, looking up into my eyes, "Mr. Cowper, how do you like my $50,000 refrigerator?" There wasn't a trace of humor in her face.

Her husband had died a few months earlier, without insurance. The tragic accident that had taken his life had left her with three mouths to feed, no income, and no savings to draw on.

"Instead of using our money for the insurance you tried to sell us," she said, "we bought this new refrigerator. Now, John is gone. I am still alone, the house still has a $50,000 mortgage and now I can't make the payments. That's why the For Sale sign is on my lawn.... That's why I say, see my $50,000 refrigerator. Do you understand?"

I almost cried with her. That was the moment when the power of insurance – and the real reason I sell it – came to me. It was the defining moment in my career. It forever changed how I saw my product, my clients and my role in their lives. Looking back on it now, although I never want to be pushy, I think I gave up too early. I should have tried to find a way around John and Maria's objection. If it hadn't been for my own weakness when faced with their objections, the mortgage would not have been called and that poor woman and her children would have kept their home.

Strategy 2: Have passion for the promise

What I learned that night was that just knowing how your products work isn't enough to sell successfully. Even in those young days, seated across from John and Maria, I knew how my policies worked. I knew all of the guarantees in the contracts, how much money the plan required and how much money they could expect at the end. But I failed them because I wasn't passionate enough about the promise that life insurance makes. I didn't know what I needed in order to protect Maria and her children. I hadn't personally experienced what could happen if I let a potential client make a poor decision. I needed the passion to sell another way – personally, and with emotion.

A policy is just a piece of paper, a contract that describes a deal I broker between a client and an insurer. But once I was able to look beyond that, I saw that what I am really selling is the promise on that piece of paper – to balance the books at a person's death and provide for their dependents. That's a powerful promise. It changes lives.

To truly prosper, salespeople have to ask themselves what it is they are selling. What is it that is so powerful about the piece of paper that a client signs? What idea is the client really responding to when they say yes, I need what you are selling? Whether the promise is a secure retirement, an early retirement or a change in lifestyle, make it your singular focus. Remember the power of the promise. Never lose sight of it, and it will guide you in all your cases. If you can remember that one piece of information, you will always do what is best for the client, and everything else will follow.

Strategy 3: Be passionate about your products

Let me tell you an old story that illustrates the importance
of passion in selling.

Romancing the stone

A man in a dark blue suit and heavy woolen overcoat stepped
off Park Avenue through the frosted glass doors of a certain very
exclusive jewelry boutique. He stomped the snow off his shoes
and paused for a moment at the front of the store to look around.
A smile came to his face as he surveyed the old joined wood and
glass cabinetry filled with sparkling diamonds, rubies and emeralds
all set in glistening gold and laid out on dark purple velvet. The
well-dressed gentleman behind the counter nodded hello and
inquired, "Sir, is there anything I can take out for you today?"

"Yes, as a matter of fact there is, my good man," replied the
customer. "Show me the large diamond in the central window
out front if you would please."

"Certainly, sir," smiled the salesman. He went to the front of the
store, unlocked the back of the window cabinet and delicately removed
the stone. He walked back to the customer and placed the gem
on the counter, so that the man could inspect it. After a few quiet
seconds the customer scratched his chin and looked up at the clerk.

"How much is it?" he asked.

"$5,400," replied the salesman.

"Hmmm."

The man re-examined the stone more carefully, then, after
a few seconds, picked his lambskin gloves up off the counter,
thanked the clerk and turned to leave the store. The owner of the
store, who had been watching the transaction from his desk in the
corner, now stepped forward and called out, "Sir! A moment please."

The man stopped just before reaching the door and swiveled
on his heel, a questioning look on his face.

"Please allow me to offer you one more glance at that precious
jewel," said the owner. "I couldn't help but notice your interest in
what is clearly the most beautiful diamond in our establishment
and I think it deserves one more viewing."

The owner reached to take the diamond from his assistant, then produced a snow white handkerchief, and lovingly polished the stone to an even more brilliant shine before placing it gently on a plush velvet cushion he had produced from beneath the counter.

"See how stunning it looks against this background," he said. "I must compliment you on your exquisite taste and I simply had to ensure that you saw this stone in its most favorable light. Notice how the light from above is refracted throughout the perfectly cut facets. It is indeed a perfect diamond that has been cut by a master. Notice the clarity and the way that it picks up the purple of the surface beneath it. How beautiful.

"Now come with me to the door and see it sparkle in the sun. Wouldn't the object of your desires melt knowing that you loved her enough to offer her such a brilliant gift, this indestructible stone of crystallized sunlight?"

The man in the blue suit, mesmerized by the quiet confidence of the owner, scratched his chin thoughtfully again. Then, placing his gloves down on the counter he said, "I'll take it."

When the diamond had been paid for and taken away to be prepared for delivery, the customer turned to the owner and asked, "Why did I buy the stone from you and not your assistant?"

"The difference is," replied the owner, "I truly love that stone."

Strategy 4: Be passionate about your business

That is the power of passion. And, just like the owner of that jewelry store, who sold the diamond because he loved it, I believe you must truly love life insurance to sell it successfully. As a veteran life insurance agent once told me, "You'll never be able to get into the life insurance business, until the life insurance business gets into you." I've already described to you the defining moment when passion for my products flooded through me. I also find the passion and confidence to sell life insurance in the history of the life insurance business.

Ever since I was a child I have been a history buff and, when I entered the life insurance business in the late fifties, I began to develop an interest in how the industry was started and how it developed. To my surprise I discovered that, far from being a dry business built on analyses of mortality tables, investment curves and interest projections, the story of life insurance describes our desire to make our mark on the world and protect our families after our deaths. It is a history of success and compassion that has only increased my passion and helped me sell with more conviction.

A proud tradition

We can trace the concept of insurance all the way back to the earliest days of our species, when the stronger members of the tribe cared for those too weak to hunt or forage. This altruistic impulse evolved through the ages and found expression in the feudal system of the Middle Ages and the growth of guilds that followed. Eventually the practice of caring for others was formalized into a business – and the insurance industry was born. In 1794, The Insurance Company of North America was founded to do a general business of insuring lives. Within 50 years, eight insurance companies were formed in America and all still operate today. In fact, insurance had become so important that during the American Civil War, New York Life, one of those original eight, would ride in under flags of truce to pay death claims to rival Confederate policyholders.

However, in addition to protecting their families, people also began to use insurance to amass great wealth. During the Roaring Twenties, when everyone else was playing the stock market, singer Rudy Vallee drew a lot of criticism for investing in insurance annuities. However, when the stock market crashed in '29 and everyone lost their shirts, Vallee, who was liquid because of his annuities, began buying up large amounts of devalued real estate at bargain-basement prices. By the time he died, he was one of the wealthiest people in the U.S. In that same period, Walt Disney financed his company by borrowing on the cash values of his and his brother's insurance policies. They had simply not been able to find a bank to lend money to an enterprise involving Mickey Mouse.

The rich history of life insurance is an inexhaustible fountain of inspiration for me. John, Maria and the past masters of insurance made my chosen profession and my products come alive for me.

73

As a result, I am able to pass along that fire and conviction to my prospects. I can always be sure of giving them the advice they need, instead of just telling them what I think they want to hear, and when we put protection in place for their families, we both become part of something more valuable than just a paper transaction.

Strategy 5: Use your passion to close cases

Over the course of my career, the $50,000 refrigerator I discussed earlier has stayed with me as a reminder of my responsibilities to my prospects and clients. I have never allowed myself to forget Maria's anguish after her husband's death and because of that memory I am determined to never conduct myself as anything less than a consummate life insurance professional. I don't browbeat my prospects into buying, but I will passionately try to make them see why they need insurance if it's in their best interests. Over the years this attitude has enabled me to help a lot of families who are at risk and has resulted in several sales that other agents may not have been able to close. In particular, I would never have made the following sale without both the passion I got from my experience with John and Maria and my personal explorations into the great tradition that life insurance was built on.

Your creditors, or your wife

I was seated in an elegant green leather chair, facing the 60-year-old owner of a Toronto shoe factory. On the walls of his office, instead of diplomas, were framed photographs of his wife and three children.

"I know you're right about my need for this insurance, Mr. Cowper," he was saying, "but, I hardly think it's fair to be spending the kind of money you're talking about when this company owes as much as it does to the bank. How can I possibly spend money on my insurance when my creditors are hungry for their return? I just don't do business that way. I'm sorry."

We argued back and forth for the better part of another fifteen minutes but I wasn't getting anywhere. I knew he was a busy man and I could see that my effort to impress him with the need for insurance was only annoying him. He had no problem understanding the need, but, like John before him, he just had other priorities. I was about to close my briefcase and say good afternoon when I remembered what had happened to John so many years ago. I couldn't let that happen again. I couldn't leave that office without plainly and firmly letting this prospect know that, in my professional opinion, his priorities were out-of-whack.

I stood up from my chair and picked up my briefcase as if to leave. Playing a Colombo routine to the hilt, I said, "Er, excuse me again, sorry to pester you but, could you just answer one more question for me?"

The man behind the desk let out an exasperated sigh. "Go ahead," he waved.

"I was just wondering, if you'll indulge me, sir, what would happen if this Sunday afternoon you went to see *The Sound of Music* with your family at the theater down the street and by some unbelievable coincidence when you find your seats you notice that every single one of your creditors was there as well? Now imagine that the lights dim, the curtains draw and the film begins. A third of the way through the film, perhaps during 'Do-re-me,' you become hungry and duck out to the lobby for popcorn. But, while you are outside a fire breaks out in the theater. You charge back into the smoke and, coughing and choking, you quickly realize that you can save only four people. Tell me, sir, who would you save, four of your creditors or your wife and three children?"

The owner hung his head low to his desk and groaned.

The check that he wrote that day ended up saving not only his wife and three children, but also his creditors.

Your defining moment

In order to break through to the most successful levels in any sales industry, I believe every salesperson needs to have some defining moment and recognize it as such. You may have already had yours, but haven't fully appreciated it. For many insurance agents it comes when delivering a death benefit to a grieving widow or helping a disabled policyholder with a much needed check. In those defining moments fear, apprehension and doubt are wiped away. We need to hold onto these moments for our entire careers and to remember them when we are with each of our prospects. They are examples of the power of our product. The passion that comes from those moments lends conviction to your words and a feeling of strength and pride to each encounter.

If our clients are troubled by an insurance need and we fail to demonstrate the importance of their potential losses, then we have failed as professionals.

Five strategies for finding the passion to close cases

1) FIND YOUR OWN PASSION.

2) HAVE PASSION FOR THE PROMISE.

3) BE PASSIONATE ABOUT YOUR PRODUCTS.

4) BE PASSIONATE ABOUT YOUR BUSINESS.

5) USE YOUR PASSION TO CLOSE CASES.

I told one

company president that he could

never be a famous secret ...

CHAPTER 5

Meet the people

Y ou've seen in chapters 3 and 4 how knowledge and passion are crucial to closing cases. They literally mean the difference between making the sale and not making the sale. They are the keys to success. However, you won't get the chance to use your knowledge and passion, unless you have prospects. As I like to say, you cannot be a famous secret.

In this chapter, I'll show you 4 strategies for meeting prospects: 1) Leverage your network to its fullest. 2) Uncover the entire market. 3) Meet the people your prospects depend on. 4) Be visible. But before we explore these strategies, let me tell you how I discovered the key to networking.

Six handshakes away from the President

In 1957, I migrated to North America with $40 in my pocket and a boatload of ambition. While on the cruise over from Scotland I spent a lot of time lounging on the deck of the ocean liner, enjoying the mid-Atlantic sun, my head filled with dreams and plans for my life in a new land of opportunity.

One day, about a week into the voyage, I was reading an article in a magazine that reported a fact that struck me immediately and was to have a lasting impact on my entire insurance career. The author of the article claimed, as a result of a study done in the United States, that even the least influential person in the smallest village in America was only six handshakes away from the President.

I put my magazine down and thought about that for a while. I was amazed that an entire country could be seen as one great web of connections, a vast network in which hobos knew soup kitchen managers, who knew welfare workers, who knew local politicians, who knew mayors, who knew local congressmen, who knew the President. Suddenly the key to networking was revealed to me. All you need is to be able to start a chain of introductions to meet powerful people. Although the continent I was moving to was an intimidating land, filled with over 200 million strangers, I resolved then to keep building a network until I was only one handshake away from the leader of the country.

Sitting on the deck, under the warm afternoon sun, I saw myself clearly, on a day not too far in the future, shaking the Prime Minister's hand. But before that happened, I would shake the hands of many thousands of prospects.

Strategy 1: Leverage your network to its fullest

When I was just starting out in the insurance business, I was forced to cold call because I had no network to draw upon for prospects. Nonetheless, I managed to survive by doing what I call 'kitchen-table seances.' I knew, however, that to become successful, I would need to start building a network. I looked around for opportunities and found one in the Ontario Medical Association Group Life Plan that my company underwrote. With this plan I could enroll doctors and be paid $25 for each enrollment. I saw it as being paid to build a network of prospects, and started calling doctors enthusiastically. For every 100 phone calls I made to doctors, I was able to enroll about 25 of them, make $625, and develop a network of doctors at the same time. But I knew that to dramatically improve my sales, I would have to leverage my network to its fullest.

To me, leveraging my network meant becoming part of the medical fraternity. Whenever I met a doctor I wanted to be able to discuss where they studied medicine, who their colleagues were and how they were doing. By appearing to be a part of their world, I knew I would gain their trust and have a better chance of making a sale.

To help me become part of my prospect's world, I picked up a stack of old medical-school yearbooks. Before going to see a particular doctor, I looked them up to find out what their interests were, what teams and clubs they had joined, and who their classmates were. Because the medical community was a relatively small one, I usually had no trouble finding classmates I had already met while doing the enrollments. Many of these former medical students had lost touch with each other over the years, so when I went to see my prospects I would always spend a few minutes filling them in on how their old friends were doing. They enjoyed the news and would often quiz me for more details. After a few minutes, my prospects were totally disarmed and comfortable with my presence. I had created an atmosphere of familiarity and trust – an atmosphere conducive to selling. Let me show you a case where leveraging my network helped me open and close a deal.

The graduate

Before I left the house in the morning I sat down with my coffee, a pen and the Ontario Medical yearbook. At 10 o'clock I had an appointment to visit Dr. Hallworthy, a pediatrician and graduate of the University of Toronto, class of '55. I quickly flipped through the pages of the yearbook until I found his picture. He wore glasses, had a slightly bent nose and a friendly smile in his black-and-white grad photo. Underneath the listing for Hallworthy, I found out that he swam competitively when he was at school, played chess and sang in a barbershop quartet. His small oval picture was surrounded by other photos of doctors in his year, including Gerry Benz, who I had enrolled and sold disability insurance to just recently. Gerry and I had talked about swimming during my visit to his office. Since he and Hallworthy were both on the swimming team, I suspected they might have been buddies – I would find out shortly.

I arrived at Dr. Hallworthy's office at 10 o'clock in the morning. He had a private general practice in a low office building in the north end of the city. His office was a fairly small cube with one window looking out from the second story over the building's parking lot. As I walked in, Dr. Hallworthy glanced up from the papers in front of him on his desk and sighed. He didn't seem too happy to see me, but that was understandable. Doctors see a lot of salespeople from drug and medical supply companies. In his mind I wasn't a patient who would be bringing in revenue, I was just another salesperson looking to rob him of a few of his hard-earned dollars.

I reached across the desk and shook his hand, "Hello, Dr. Hallworthy."

"Have a seat," he said, gesturing to the chair on my side of the desk.

As I sat down I glanced quickly around the room and saw his graduation photo and diploma proudly displayed. Beside them, I was happy to see the same set of medals Gerry Benz had hanging from his wall.

"Do you know Gerry Benz?" I asked.

He looked up at me over his glasses. "Yeah, we went to school together, why?" he asked, curious about my odd approach and probably wondering how I knew his old classmate. With that one simple question I'd already differentiated myself from all of the other salespeople who walked into his office.

"I saw him four weeks ago. He has an ear-nose-and-throat practice in Scarborough."

"Really? I'd wondered where Gerry got to. I always meant to keep in touch, but you get so busy."

"I can certainly appreciate that. Gerry was saying that he barely even has time for a swim any more."

"Oh, I know. Gerry and I were on the school team together, you know."

"Really? Well I swim myself, but not competitively of course," I said with a laugh.

"Actually, Gerry bought a disability policy from me when I was there. He was joking that he didn't know which would be worse, being too injured to work or too injured to swim."

"Yeah, tough choice," said Dr. Hallworthy, "although I'm pretty sure I know what my wife would say."

I had never actually said that Gerry recommended me to Dr. Hallworthy, but Hallworthy clearly was beginning to regard me as trustworthy. If Gerry hadn't thrown me out I must have something worth listening to.

"Speaking of your wife, do you have life and disability insurance to protect your family in the event of your death or injury?"

When I entered Dr. Hallworthy's office I had been a stranger he was reluctant to see, but during the meeting I established myself as part of his circle of friends. By the time I left, he had purchased life and disability insurance.

Strategy 2: Uncover the entire market

Over a period of months, I had called on most of the doctors in my area and had begun to wonder if I had saturated the market. I had gained a lot of experience dealing with doctors, and I didn't want it to go to waste, but I wondered if I should start looking for new markets. But before doing this, I knew I had to be certain that I had uncovered the entire market.

When I asked myself whether or not I had truly called on most of the doctors in my area, I realized that the answer was no. I had called doctors who worked during the day, but what about the ones who worked the graveyard shift? Saving lives is a 24-hour-a-day business – there must have been hundreds of night-shift doctors who had never been approached by an agent. They were an untapped market. So, like these doctors, I started working the night shift.

I quickly developed a very feline, but productive method of working. I would rise early in the morning, as is my natural habit, and head off to the office to take care of my paperwork. In the early afternoon I would either call or visit the local hospitals to look for prospects. Then, usually exhausted, I would slip home for a few hours sleep before seeing doctors in the wee hours of the morning.

Let me show you one of my night-time cases.

The graveyard shift

Monday morning I rose at my usual time, ate breakfast and was out of the house by 9:00 AM. I drove out to the Toronto Northern Hospital to start generating some leads for that evening.

I entered the lobby of the massive stone building, and stopped for a moment to look around. The floors were marble tile. Shiny silver elevators came and went to my right, relatives of patients sat in rows to my left, and ahead of me, behind a large circular information desk, a huge directory to the entire hospital was hung on the wall.

Taking out a pen and paper, I wrote down the name of every doctor working in the hospital. That list would become my prospecting schedule for the day.

From the hospital I went straight to my office and got on the phone. For the balance of the morning, I made call after call into that hospital's switchboard, asking for one doctor after another and making a note beside the names of those working the late shift. I would call them later in the evening.

Setting up the appointment

"Hello, Dr. Sokol," I began, "I'm with the New York life Insurance Company and I'm rolling out a new program we've developed for obstetricians. I understand you're on call this evening?"

"Well, yes," he replied, unsure how to respond, "I spend my evenings here waiting for pregnant mothers to go into labor."

"I can't imagine a more rewarding career, even if you do have to work through the night," I said. "I was wondering if I could drop by and see you to discuss the products we're providing for your profession."

"Well, I may get called away."

"That's okay," I replied, "I'll come at 11:00. We can sit and talk. At the very least I'll bring coffee and keep you company. If you get called away, I don't mind."

The sell

Dr. Sokol was waiting for me when I arrived at the little cubicle he used between calls. I handed him a cup of coffee and squeezed into a chair very close to him. The green walls pressed in on us. It was like being in a closet.

"Thanks for the coffee," he said, "I hope I didn't drag you out here at this ungodly hour for nothing, but, you know, I've been thinking about the idea of you taking the money I earn while I'm alive and hanging on to it until after I'm dead and I don't really feel very good about that."

"Well, that's a perfectly good reason for not buying insurance, but insurance is not a product that only provides a return after you're dead. It can be a very effective tool for building your retirement income. You could really look at it as a plan for setting aside funds for your retirement. The product will, in fact, guarantee a competitive rate of return on your money. Let me ask you how many patients you treat in an evening?"

"Maybe 8 or 10," he replied.

"One day," I said, "your patients will retire you, but they won't pension you. For every 3 patients that walk through your door now, you do one for the government, one for the cost of running your practice, and one for yourself. It never gets better – in fact, it gets worse. Why don't you take 2 or 3 of those patients everyday and send them ahead for yourself so you can move from temporary income to permanent income.

"Whether it's here at the hospital, or at your home," I continued, "you're going to see an awful lot of salespeople over the course of your career. They're all going ask you to spend your money. I may be the only one you ever see who asks you to save it."

"I never thought of it like that," Dr. Sokol said, "but I have investments already."

"Yes, but what if you die before you manage to save enough to take care of your family? Insurance is a unique financial tool that can both provide for your retirement should you live long enough, and provide for your dependents should you die too soon. I know the subject of your own mortality is not an appealing one, but it is not one you can avoid. It's just like your practice. You see a half dozen women every night who weren't pregnant nine months ago. General practitioners see patients every day who were not sick two weeks before, and funeral directors are fitting caskets for people who had no idea, six months ago, that they would be dead today."

"Sure, but I am a doctor and a very healthy man," he replied. "Why would I need insurance now?"

A money machine

"Think about it this way," I said, "imagine your wife was managing your affairs. You are a business that she runs. Now, you're bringing in $100,000 a year in income for her. You are, in fact, the sole source of income for this company she runs. But let's say you were a machine not a human being. It's as if she had a machine in your basement at home that produced dollar bills. Whenever she needed the cash she could go down there and crank out another handful, up to a total of $100,000 a year. Even though she keeps the machine locked up in your dry, insulated basement, and it is so well-made it will probably last for years, there's no doubt in my mind she would be doing everything in her power to have it insured in case it broke down.

"Now imagine that machine was being driven all over the city every day. It left the house in the evening and came home in the morning just like you. That machine is at risk, anything could happen. Anything could happen to you – a car accident, a mugging, an illness. Why isn't she trying to get you insured?"

Dr. Sokol shrugged.

"Because she thinks you're taking care of that. She's taking care of the expenses and the house and your children. I'm sure she doesn't foresee a day when the money will stop flowing. Why should she? She thinks you're making sure it will last forever, and you're too busy trying to take care of these pregnant women to worry about that. You're both doing a great job, but your future is falling through the cracks."

Now I had his interest. "I see what you mean," he said, biting his lip.

"That home you live in – do you consider that a home for your family as long as you live?"

"Of course I do," he stammered. "We've lived there over 20 years."

"Why don't you see it as being a home for your family as long as *they* live then?"

"You're saying that if I die they'll lose the house, right?" he asked.

"Very likely," I nodded, "and they will certainly suffer a drastic change in their lifestyle if you die and leave them nothing."

Adding a zero

"If we did this insurance," he asked, "how much would it cost?"

"Well, I'd have to look at your situation in a little more detail to give you a firm figure, but as I said, we're talking about putting aside a few percent of your income to secure you and your family's future."

He thought about it again and then said, "How much would $200,000 cost?"

"Why do you bring that figure up?" I asked.

"I think that would cover what's left of the mortgage and leave my wife and kids in a good position," he said.

"That may be true, Dr. Sokol," I replied, "but let's look at that in more detail. What if I were to ask to buy your business from you?"

"How much would you give me for it?" he asked.

"Well, you've already established the price. I'd offer $200,000," I said, smiling.

"What?!" he cried. "My practice makes almost that much in two years. That's crazy."

"Exactly," I said. "You'll earn $1 million dollars before you retire in 10 years. Dr. Sokol, I'd like to insure you against the loss of that income, because the loss of $1 million would be the impact your death would have on your wife and children, aside from the emotional trauma of course. Remember, if you leave here tomorrow morning and get into an accident on your way home, your wife and children are giving up $1 million, not $200,000 as you suggest."

Dr. Sokol was not convinced he needed $1 million of insurance, but he did agree to purchase a policy for $300,000 – considerably more insurance then he had earlier in the evening, so I was satisfied that I had protected Dr. Sokol's family to the best of my abilities.

Riding the real estate boom

The period in my life when I sold to doctors had been a great time for me. It allowed me to move beyond pure survival and add the first of many zeroes to my average policy size. But then the Ontario government stepped in and instituted a plan to provide free health care to its citizens. This put a cap on a doctor's salary and, effectively, limited my own earning power. Although I was doing well financially, I realized it was time to move from the medical market and apply the networking and sales skills I'd learned in the past few years to an industry that was actually booming, instead of dying, as a result of government policies.

On that first day I spent in Toronto in 1957, walking up University Avenue, the ceaseless construction had captured my attention and imagination. Since then I had harbored a secret passion to be involved in what seemed like an exciting business. Because the government was actively encouraging – with favorable planning rules and tax breaks – the building boom exploding through the city, I decided to jump on the bandwagon. The lucrative and high-stakes real estate development market would be my next target.

Strategy 3: Meet the people your prospects depend on

I didn't know any developers and there was no enrollment plan for them, so I would have to create my network from scratch. Unfortunately, developers were not easy to meet. They were private and moved in different circles. I figured that if I couldn't meet them directly, I would have to look for people to introduce me to them. In other words, I would have to get to know the people they depended on. When I looked into how developers work, I realized they rely heavily on politicians, because their developments have to pass through zoning meetings, planning boards, various government levels and departments. A development could grind to a halt because of bureaucratic antagonism anywhere along the way. Clearly, it was in a developer's interest to have politicians on their side, and if I knew the politicians, I would be able to get to know the developers. I could become a resource for them, and open doors – that would be my value added. Fortunately, because politicians were public figures, not private business people, they were easier to meet. Let me tell you the story of how I got started in politics.

Getting started in politics

Since I wasn't yet a citizen of Canada I had no real choice other than to start at the bottom of the ladder. I couldn't run for political office, so I decided to help by canvassing for a local alderman. I was excited about participating at a municipal level, because municipal politics have by far the greatest impact on our daily lives. The city government makes sure our garbage is picked up, our sidewalk isn't crumbling and our water is drinkable. I've always felt that if I live in a democratic country and enjoy all the benefits that go along with that, I have a responsibility to participate in the democratic process. It was long, sometimes thankless work, but I put as much effort into it as I did selling insurance. I was fascinated by the campaign process – we had to start up and tear down three different organizations, one to run the election, one for advertising, and one just to manage the election day. Eventually I got to know everyone on the campaign and earned a good reputation because of my drive.

The city planning board

Over the years I worked my way up through the party structure. Eventually, I was asked to manage a campaign for a local candidate. We won and I went on to manage nine successful municipal, provincial and federal campaigns. At the end of that long political ride, I had made enough of the right connections to finally ask for what I needed – a position on the city planning board, where I would have a ringside seat to all the development activity.

When an opening came up on the planning board I put my name forward at city hall. Being appointed to the board in 1969 gave me the ability to see, firsthand, the issues developers were facing and gave me an opportunity to meet with them on a regular basis. My appointment was for three years and during that period I gained an understanding of the developers' business. I was able to assess their opportunities and problems, and appreciate their need to expand. After I left the planning board, I was finally able to approach the developers I had met. In the next chapter, I will show you some of the megacases I did with developers.

Strategy 4: Be visible

I seem to be something of an oxymoron: both shy and extroverted. Although I enjoy staying home, I know that in order to build my network, I have to be active socially. As I always say, you can't be a famous secret. So I make the effort to get involved in various community activities, such as political causes I believe in or my favorite charities.

Associating yourself with organizations that have credibility and prestige will greatly increase the odds that prospects will talk to you because they want to be associated with whatever you are doing. For instance, I would always take a certain block of time out of my schedule in the Spring of every year to do charity work. For a long time, this meant working for the Cancer Society. I canvassed for them, raising funds in their annual charity drives and eventually became president of the Toronto Chapter. One of the side benefits to this, along with the satisfaction of helping so many people, was the people I met along the way. I had to make hundreds of calls to prominent citizens who had been successful in almost every line of work. To them I was a humanitarian not a salesman.

As well, when I was working the campaign trail with my political candidates I used to organize dinners at which they would be keynote speakers. Anyone can do this. You don't have to be a campaign manager. Round up some speakers, give the dinner a theme and start inviting the people you want to meet. I found that most of the people I invited would attend. They didn't know me from Adam but they were very interested in what my speakers had to say. When the 18 or 20 guests were seated they would find envelopes in front of them containing the names of everyone attending, their profession or position in their company and where they were seated. That way everyone had a chance to network. Those evenings were such a success I began receiving requests from people to organize one for them. One architect I knew met most of the city's developers at such dinners. I told one insurance company president that he could never be a 'famous secret' and he really should try to increase his profile in the business community. I put on one of those dinners for him and he was able to meet the movers and shakers – chairpersons of legal firms, senior partners in accounting firms, mayors and other bigwigs. Of course, after that evening I was able to call those people up myself and invite them to a private luncheon to talk about the kind of business I do.

Context is everything

I use breakfast, lunch and dinner as great reasons to get together with even the remotest of strangers in a comfortable, relaxing atmosphere. There is no doubt that great food served in an upscale venue promotes good conversation. I can learn more about a prospect over a meal than I ever could in a one-hour meeting at their office. People just open up a lot more in a restaurant's intimate surroundings. That's why, for years, I kept a corner table at the Park Plaza dining room and a table at Winston's, long one of Toronto's finest restaurants.

I had breakfast every morning at the Park Plaza and often met politicians and lawyers who were seated at adjoining tables. Winston's was such an exclusive place that when I invited prospects to dinner there, they almost never turned me down. Certainly, I benefited from the aura of those venues. When I was made chairman of the fund-raising committee for the Toronto Cancer Society, I initiated a series of business breakfasts. In fact, at the time, the Toronto Star billed me as the 'Founder of the Business Breakfast.' The Cancer Society was used to having luncheons, but a 2-hour meal cut the heart out of the day, and too many people canceled at the last minute to take care of sudden business issues. By switching to a business breakfast, people could still be in their office by 9:00 AM. This virtually eliminated the no-shows.

The handshake of my life

On a rainy evening in 1980 I reached a target I had set for myself almost twenty years before.

The event was a benefit for the Cancer Society. We had organized an evening that featured the premiere of *Tribute*, a film starring Jack Lemmon as a terminal cancer patient. Prior to the screening, there was a cast party at The Four Seasons Hotel, and afterwards, a buffet dinner. Tickets were sold for $500 a person.

At the party, my wife Teri and I took our seats at the head table in the main ballroom of the hotel, and chatted with the senators and business leaders who were seated nearby. I was in high spirits. Everyone was enthusiastic about the evening and we knew the Cancer Society would enjoy a huge windfall from our efforts. Midway through the party, I looked up from a conversation I was having and suddenly realized we were surrounded by a phalanx of official-looking men in blue suits. For a brief second I wondered what was going on, then the suits parted, and seated one seat away from me was Pierre Trudeau, our Prime Minister.

Not only did I shake hands with the Prime Minister that night, but we raised a six-figure amount for the Cancer Society – which shows that meeting people and helping people do not have to be mutually exclusive activities.

Meeting the Prime Minister was not the primary purpose of that evening, and I certainly didn't sell him any insurance. But, shaking his hand symbolized how extensive my network had become. If I'm shaking the Prime Minister's hand, I must also be shaking the hands of a lot of power players along the way – people with insurance needs much greater than the doctors I had been working with previously. If you are going to add extra zeroes and move toward megacases, you need to build a wide and effective network.

Four strategies for meeting the people

1) LEVERAGE YOUR NETWORK TO ITS FULLEST.

2) UNCOVER THE ENTIRE MARKET.

3) MEET THE PEOPLE YOUR PROSPECTS DEPEND ON.

4) BE VISIBLE.

I could get inside their

psyches and see what

they wanted out of life and how

I could help them achieve their dreams.

In fact, back in those days,

I often referred to myself as

a merchant of dreams.

CHAPTER 6

Understand your prospects

Developing strategies for meeting people was certainly a boost to my career, but I wouldn't have been able to close sales had I not understood my prospects. There are lots of different reasons why people need insurance, and each market has its own peculiarities. My goal was to understand those peculiarities better than any other insurance agent. In order to meet this goal, I developed 3 essential strategies: 1) Get inside your prospect's psyche. 2) Learn your prospect's business. 3) Understand your prospect's risks.

In this chapter, I'll show you some challenging cases where I used these strategies to make the sale, and how I eventually managed to achieve my goal of adding another zero to the size of the policies I was writing. Instead of selling hundred-thousand-dollar policies to doctors, I was soon selling multi-million-dollar policies to developers and builders on a regular basis.

Strategy 1: Get inside your prospect's psyche

I first learned how important it was to understand my prospects during my first year in the business, long before I was selling to doctors or developers. Because I had been an interior decorator for years before entering the insurance business, I knew what it was like to be a subcontractor, to work long, demanding hours. Back in Scotland, one of my specialties had been carving imitation wood grains into the varnishes on plywood doors and walls. I would often work in uncomfortable, precarious positions, lying on my stomach while etching baseboards, or balancing myself on top of a ladder to finish the molding on a door frame. My neck would ache and my hands would cramp up. It was truly exhausting. The older guys I worked with, with their sore backs and stiff limbs, were reminders to us younger fellas that we wouldn't be able to do this kind of work forever. It was no surprise that we all dreamed of the day when we could stop working. Retiring was on our minds more than it was for our cohorts who had paper-pushing jobs. Later, as an insurance agent, I knew I could help turn those dreams into reality.

So I went after subcontractors.

Kyle's accumulation plan

With all the building and renovating going on in the city, subcontractors weren't hard to find. All I had to do was drive around and look for the trucks and vans. One afternoon, I took a tour of the lakefront area and saw that Humphrey's, an old industrial building, was being refurbished. I pulled my Buick up to the front and got out. There was lots of activity inside and I was eager to approach some of the workmen.

As I marched through the front doors, with my briefcase at my side, I heard a security guard call out, "Hey, you!"

I stopped in my tracks. Ahead, through the doors, I saw a couple of men sitting down on a bench, obviously on break. I had to find a way to speak to them.

"Where do you think you're going?" he asked.

"Inside to speak with the workmen."

"Yeah, and who are you?"

I had no other choice. "Union sent me."

"All right," he said, as he waved me in.

I walked toward the two men on break. "Hey, you," I said, trying to sound authoritative. I wanted their attention, and I didn't think the smooth-talking-salesman approach was going to work on these guys.

"What?" said one of the men.

"I'm here to talk about your retirement," I replied. "Let me take you to lunch across the street and change your life."

"I brought my lunch," he replied.

"I didn't," said the other guy sitting beside him. "If you're buying lunch, I'm coming." He stood up.

"David Cowper," I said to him.

"Kyle Carruthers," he said, in a thick Scottish accent.

"Glasgow?" I asked.

"Yeah, you?"

"Edinburgh," I replied.

"We're still kicking your backside in football, aye."

"Aye, aye," I replied, dialing up my accent a little more now.

Big things to talk about

We walked across the street together and headed into the diner. "I'm famished, ya know," Kyle said.

"Whatever you like," I replied. "Eat big, Kyle, 'cause we've got big things to talk about."

Kyle ordered enough for two. His bill alone would mean I had to make a sale.

We chatted a little bit more about football, and other things Scottish, like lassies. Kyle seemed relaxed, and I decided to steer the conversation toward a sale. "Kyle, let me ask you something. How long have you been working as a subcontractor?"

"Too long," he replied.

"So, what's your plan?" I asked.

"What plan?"

"I mean, you can't keep working like this forever."

"That's for sure."

"So, how are you going to stop working one day?"

"Don't know really. Government, I guess."

"You know, the government doesn't take care of subcontractors the same way they do back in Glasgow."

"What do ya mean?" he asked.

"I mean, they don't have the pensions here that the guys back home are going to get."

"How come?"

"That's just the way it is now. Here, they expect you to take care of yourself."

"And how's a guy supposed to do that?"

I paused for a moment, allowing Kyle to meditate on his question.

"Kyle," I said, "let's say you start a savings plan now. How much money could you put away each month?"

"I don't know," he replied.

"A thousand dollars?" I asked.

He guffawed.

"A dollar?"

Now he sniggered.

"Okay, somewhere between a thousand dollars and one dollar is what you could put away. So is it about forty dollars, or so?" I asked.

"Twenty-five, I guess," he said.

"Okay, now what kind of plan would you like to put that twenty-five dollars into? Let's say you could design your own savings plan, one that will do everything possible to help you retire. What would you like that plan to do?"

"What do you mean?" he asked.

"I mean, tell me all the things you'd like to see in a savings plan. For example," I said, "you'd want a decent return on your money."

"That's for sure."

"And what else?"

"I don't know, what else can you get in a plan?" he asked. As I had expected, Kyle hadn't put much thought into how he was going to provide for his retirement. I could have simply told him what features my plan had, but that wouldn't have had much impact on him. I wanted him to really think about the benefits of the plan I was proposing, and how they would affect his life.

Disarmed and disabled

"What if you hurt yourself and can't go to work?" I continued. "If you can't work, you won't be earning money. And if you're not earning money, how can you put aside money in your savings plan?"

"I guess I can't," he replied.

"But wouldn't you want to design your plan so that if you couldn't work, your plan still grew as if you were still making your payments?"

"Yeah, of course."

"And you'd want money available in the plan in case of an opportunity or an emergency, wouldn't you?" He nodded. "And enough money in the plan for when you retire." He nodded again. "And in case you die somewhere along your path toward retirement, the plan should complete itself instantly and pay to your family all the money you set out to save." A curious look came over his face.

I repeated the concept to him. "If it turns out that you aren't around long enough to save all the money you planned to save, this plan will complete itself when you die."

His eyes opened wide. "Is this life insurance?" he asked suspiciously.

"Of course it is," I replied. "If you die, your family will receive a death benefit. Let me explain it this way – you want a savings plan that addresses the issue of time. Time is what life is made of. And all of us have only a limited amount of it. Some of us will die too soon, some of us will live too long, but we all die in the end. The best savings plan should take care of all possibilities." I paused, while he considered what I was saying, then continued. "What about the possibility that someday you get tired of working these long days. Let's say you're sick of coming home with a sore back, and decide you want to open up your own business where you can work for yourself and where you don't have to do so much physical work," I waited, prompting him for a response.

"I'd like to do that, sure."

"You'd probably have to go to a bank to get a loan, and the banker will want to know what kind of guy you are. He'll want to know that you're responsible enough to make payments. If you have this plan we're talking about, you'll be able to show him your savings plan and say that you've been making these monthly payments for years. The banker will be impressed. Plus, if you wanted, you could take a loan out on your very own savings – even start your business.... Now wouldn't the kind of plan you'd like have all these benefits we're talking about?"

"Yeah, but what if I can't make those payments some month?"

"Can you make the payment this month?" I asked.

"Yes," he replied.

"And the next month?"

"Yes."

"And how about the month after that?"

"Yes, I guess so. But I don't know if I'll be able to, say, in six months."

"What's happening in six months?"

"I don't know."

"Okay, say you had to drive out to Scarborough at night to see a friend. You switch on the headlights. How far can you see?"

"About 200 yards, I guess."

"So you don't switch on the lights and see all the way
to Scarborough?"

"No, of course not."

"Right," I said. "But, you'll get into your car, here, and start
driving. And from here, you'll be able to see down the street a few
blocks, but no further. But when you drive down those few blocks,
you'll be able to see another few blocks, and another few blocks
after that, and so on, until when you get close to Scarborough, you'll
be able to see the rest of the way there." I watched him looking
back at me, his eyes filling with understanding. "It's the same in
life," I added. "You can look a few months ahead now, and that's it,
but in a few months you'll see another few months in front of you."

"I see," he said.

"I have that very plan you just designed here in my briefcase."

He bought a life insurance policy from me, right there at the
table. And later in the week, I arranged to see his co-worker, and
sold him too.

I sold both of them, and many other subcontractors, because
I understood them. I knew what it was like to be them. I could get
inside their psyches and see what they wanted out of life and how
I could help them achieve their dreams. In fact, back in those days,
I often referred to myself as a merchant of dreams.

The strategy of getting inside your prospect's psyche is the key to
selling. When I was selling to subcontractors I was able to get inside
their psyches, because I understood their business and their risks. If
you do not understand your prospect's business or their risks, you
will not be able to get inside their psyches. That is why I have
developed the next two strategies.

Strategy 2: Learn your prospect's business

In chapter 5, I told you I wanted to start selling to developers. So, to
begin getting inside their psyches, I threw myself into the developers'
business. I read everything I could get my hands on about development,
I picked the brains of anyone I ran into who was at all connected

to developers, and, of course, I absorbed a tremendous amount of knowledge while I sat on the City Planning Board. Eventually I felt I understood the development business enough to know how I could help them. Let me show you briefly what I learned.

What I learned about the development business

On the planning board, I had a ringside seat to the latest projects being presented by the city's developers. What amazed me was how incredibly long and tedious the approval process was. There was an unbelievable amount of red tape and a lot of head-butting with local politicians and bureaucrats. The developers had to overcome an endless string of concerns from the politicians. How is the new development going to affect the traffic in the area? Are the local residents going to be happy about another huge building going up in their area? Is it going to destroy the peace of the neighborhood? Each of these and hundreds and sometimes thousands of other issues had to be carefully addressed. When I saw the complexity of the process, I was amazed that any new buildings went up at all.

I was stunned by the dollar amounts that were tossed around. Even before building started, the developers had to buy or option the land, pay for in-depth market studies, soil studies, design a plan based on those studies, and stay liquid throughout the entire approval process. Then, when construction did begin, the costs became horrendous. That's when millions of dollars were shelled out for architects, materials, construction equipment, the project management team, construction workers, landscape architects, electrical engineers, designers, painters, and a cast of thousands.

You'll see in the stories coming up in this chapter that my ability to talk to developers fluently about their business helped immensely in making the sales. They feel comfortable discussing their affairs with someone who understands. I don't have to burden my prospects with time- consuming questions about their industry. Instead, I can add value right away.

Strategy 3: Understand your prospect's risks

To completely get inside my prospect's psyche, I not only had to understand their business, I had to understand their risks. In order to discover the nature of their risks, I explored how the developers managed to finance projects of such incredible size. They would use existing assets to secure short-term financing until the building was complete, then they would free up their assets by taking out a mortgage on the new building, which they would eventually lease out. In some cases the projects were so large the financing was done through bond issues. By constantly leveraging old deals for new like that, they were able to take advantage of more and more investment opportunities, but each new deal they got into seemed thinner than the last one, and even though the returns were often mind-boggling, whenever they realized a profit, they preferred to reinvest in new projects rather than pay off the loans or any taxes on their gain. I knew that this incredible rate of development meant one thing – they had massive exposure to debt and taxes. Their credit would have to be underpinned.

Inside the developer's psyche

Now, having learned their business and where their risks were, I had to get inside the developer's psyche. I asked myself what kind of person initiates such massive projects, and has the ability to continue fighting for a project month after month and endure the many bleak periods when it looks like their proposal is certain to get quashed? And what kind of person assumes so much debt? I looked closely at these people and noticed a few outstanding characteristics. I first realized that they were people with incredible powers of imagination. They could drive down a street, look at an empty lot or an old building and see in its place an office tower giving employment to 20,000 people. But they had more than imagination; they had the conviction and the patience to translate their ideas onto paper and then into steel and concrete. And then, of course, they had cast-iron stomachs that allowed them to take such big risks. In other words, these developers were willing to put everything on the line to realize their dreams.

So, with this picture of a developer in mind, I figured out how I would make my approach. My goal was to show them the possible ramifications of their total dedication to their dreams. To do this, I would – as I like to say – introduce the topic of death into the economic equation of their lives. I would explain death in terms of time, in the same way I explained it to subcontractors many years before. Their developments had such faraway time horizons; they couldn't afford not to address the issue of death. Given enough time, they would probably be all right. But, because they were constantly initiating new projects, there was no end to the risk. They were always exposed, and this exposure put their families at risk. Because they were essential players in the projects, their deaths would seriously jeopardize the developments. Calling the debts would hamstring the other key people involved and leave the deceased's executors with some tough problems to solve.

Obviously, if the developer didn't care about the mess he might leave his heirs, there wasn't much I could do. But, if he did care, I knew I had the best solution to his problem, so I went around looking for the developers who believed, as I do, that a debt should never last any longer than the person who created it. Let me take you through a couple of cases to show you how I was able to leverage my understanding of my prospects' business, their risks, and their psyches. The first story is a glimpse into the typical approach I would make to developers.

Howell: the eliminate-debt-at-death-policy

I first met Norm Howell, president of Howell Capital, a small development company, when he made a presentation to the City Planning Board. And then, after I left the board, I ran into him a couple of times socially. One evening I happened to run into him at a restaurant when we were seated at adjacent tables. I reminded him who I was, and we chatted very briefly about what he was up to. In the course of our short conversation, he said he was trying to put together a plan to build a small strip mall in the suburbs.

A year or so later, I ran into him again on the street. The one thing I remembered about our restaurant meeting was his strip mall. I make a point of remembering business details like that. When I asked him how the deal was going, he said he had just received approval for it a couple of months ago. I told him I was familiar with the development business and asked if I could come see him the following week to talk about his situation and see if there was anything he might need me for. He said that would be okay and I should call his secretary later in the day to set up an appointment.

The following week I arrived at his office.

"Hi, Norm," I said as I took a seat across from his desk, "how are you?"

"A little wigged-out," he replied wearily. "It's been a hectic week. I don't really have a lot of time to spend today – maybe we should reschedule."

"How much time do you have?" I asked politely.

He glanced down at his watch. "Twenty minutes, no more, sorry."

"Okay, we'll spend twenty minutes – no more. That's probably all we really need, anyway," I said. He smiled, relieved that I wasn't pushing for more of his time. "Let me just ask you a couple of questions. I guess there are a few key people involved in this project other than yourself. Can you tell me a little bit about who's involved?"

He quickly told me that he and three other entrepreneurs were partners in the deal.

"And how have you put up the capital for the mall?" I asked.

"The bank. We mortgaged some properties, and took the rest in a business loan."

"What's the size of the loan?"

"$900,000."

Now it was time for the question that I opened my developer cases with, and still use to this day to open all my businesses cases. "How many times did you sign for the loan?" I asked.

"What do you mean by that?" he replied.

"I assume you have signed corporately for the loan as president of Howell Capital?"

"Of course," he answered.

"And personally as well?" I asked.

"Yes, I suppose I did," he said, wondering where I was going.

"You see, with that second signature of yours, the bank has blueprinted itself into a fail-safe position."

"How do you mean?"

"It's common practice for banks to ask for that second signature. Because they usually require collateral for twice the size of the loan, they want to make sure they can go after the personal estates of the corporate signatories. They need those personal guarantees for that."

I was able to speak confidently to Norm because of my knowledge of the development business and how developers finance their projects. I knew that in a privately held company the answer to the question of the second signature is invariably yes. By putting themselves in this fail-safe position, the banks simultaneously blueprint the borrower for failure, so I see it as my job to protect the borrower.

I informed Norm about the risk he had taken in signing twice. "Norm," I said, "you may not own 100% of the development project, but you are now 100% liable for the risk. Not only are 100% of your corporate assets on the line, but 100% of your non-corporate assets are on the line. Your banker, not your family, is the first beneficiary of your estate. What you've done with your personal assets is leave them as 'hostages to fate.'" I glanced down at my watch. "Norm," I continued, "twenty minutes is up."

He looked down at his own watch then looked up at me. "It'll wait," he grumbled. "I plan on paying off that loan long before my estate becomes an issue."

Introducing the topic of death into the equation of Norm's business transactions

"Norm," I said, "my job is to introduce the topic of death into the equation of your business transactions. The reality is that no one dies at the beginning of something nor at the end of something, but usually in the middle of something. And that's what we have to protect ourselves against. You've obviously put a great deal of time into this project and all your other projects. You certainly have shown a great deal of responsibility in seeing your projects through to completion. But truthfully, these projects are bigger than you. You're creating something that will last years beyond your own life. Others depend on you. Your partners, the people that will shop and work at your mall, and, much more importantly, your family. Surely your responsibility to them extends further than your own life. You don't want everything to unravel the moment you die." I paused while he considered what I was saying. I could see by his rapt expression that I was getting through to him.

"If you die with the loan outstanding," I continued, "the loan agreement becomes a lethal weapon in the hands of your banker. They'll look at your estate, and see what they can take."

"Well, David," he said, "I certainly don't want to hang my family out to dry. But we need the loan. It's not like we can finance the development without it. I've accepted the loan as part of the risk of doing my business."

"Yes, certainly, but there are ways to reduce that risk."

He leaned into his desk, his eyes focused on me. "I suppose you're going to try and sell me some life insurance," he said. "You know, I have some already."

Stand-by credit

"Let me explain it like this. Let's pretend for a moment that I'm your banker. I come in here and say to you that we'd like to offer you a special deal we're offering all our valued customers. We call it stand-by credit. We'll charge you another one percent interest a year and set aside for you $900,000 of stand-by credit, so that when you die, and the loan has to be settled, we'll automatically lend you that $900,000. Then, because you are such a good customer, we have come up with yet another idea. We will charge you another one percent interest in exchange for which we will forgive the $900,000 loan the moment we make it. Which means, of course, we won't have to resort to your estate." I let him mull the offer over. "Would you turn down that offer if the bank made it to you?"

"No, I suppose I wouldn't," he replied.

"That's precisely the offer I'm making you. It's called the eliminate-debt-at-death policy."

Money is my commodity

I look at life insurance in the same way that a banker looks at money. We're both in the money business, but we're in different branches. Money is the banker's commodity and interest is the price of that commodity. He gives his clients capital and charges them interest while they rent his capital. I do the same thing. I charge my clients interest in the form of premiums. The capital is the death benefit. The difference between the banker and me is the banker wants his capital back.

By understanding the risks Norm was taking and by appealing to his sense of responsibility I was able to make my sale. When Norm agreed to increase his interest payments by a couple of percent and secure his estate from possible ravage in the future, I came very close to my goal of adding another zero to the policy size.

The Substitute Creditor

I should add here that many of the cases I would eventually do for developers were structured on the Substitute Creditor concept, which, as you saw in chapter 3, was the idea that sparked a deal that eventually led to my $100 million case. As I mentioned then, we will be exploring how I developed the concept and what it means in chapter 11.

Not all developers are alike though. Soon after seeing Norm, I landed a case where the developers had sizable assets and, instead of being exposed to debt like Norm, were massively exposed to taxes. At the time, this case was the biggest case I had worked on. The tax liability was in the millions of dollars, which meant I would be able to add another zero to the size of my policies. And only my thorough under-standing of the development business would get me through to a close.

Lindrum, Weirnicke, and Bantam: eliminate-taxes-at-death policy

By 1970, I had realized one of my dreams – having a family. I married my wife, Teri, in 1964 and between 1965 and 1970 we had four kids. We were pushing the capacity limit on our little starter home we had purchased in the '60s, and so, in the early '70s, I decided to sell it and rent a larger town house from some landlords I had met while on the City Planning Board. As one of their tenants I had fairly frequent contact with them, and when I felt I could approach them comfortably about insurance, I asked for an appointment. They agreed and we met one afternoon at their offices on the penthouse floor of one of their buildings.

They were all there, Mr. and Mrs. Lindrum, Mr. and Mrs. Weirnicke, and Mr. and Mrs. Bantam. We all took seats around the large coffee table. From my chair I could see out of one of the large windows that overlooked the city. It was a beautiful Spring day, the sky cloudless, the air clear and crisp. I started the meeting by asking them to describe their business for me, what kind of financial condition they were in, what kind of assets and liabilities they had. After a few minutes I discovered that they had a lot of assets and were indeed millionaires. But they were millionaires in assets, not cash, and I've learned that whenever someone is a millionaire in assets, they will need me.

Unlike many of the other developers I would work with they were not very aggressive. They were careful not to overextend themselves, but because the times were very good to developers, they nonetheless had managed to amass a fair number of very lucrative properties. With the income from those properties they paid off loans and built up equity. I clearly had a different set of people in front of me – a group of conservative risk takers. My approach would have to appeal to their conservative nature.

After a while, I said, "You've all obviously managed to build an impressive portfolio of properties, which have grown considerably since you purchased them, and which will, no doubt, continue to grow in the future, but you now have a tax problem to consider. When you die, taxes will be due, and the size of the tax bill will be based on the size of your assets at your deaths. So, the question is, how will you pay those taxes? Your wealth is not in liquid cash, it's in the form of equity in your properties."

By my estimation, each of these six people required insurance for a million dollars. I had yet to sell a million dollar policy, but if I could secure this case, I would be selling six one-million-dollar policies in one fell swoop. I was eager to push on.

The 3 ways to pay off a debt at death

1. Borrowing

Mr. Lindrum, who sat across from me, and was the most vocal of the group, said, "Obviously we can pay our taxes by borrowing against our assets." He said it with a great deal of confidence, as though he had already decided long ago that that was how he would pay the inevitable taxes due on his death. Unfortunately for him, whenever someone trots out the old bromide that they can borrow against their assets I am instantly transported into a state of ecstasy. Borrowing is the most costly and a very inefficient way to pay one's taxes.

"I'm sure you can," I said, "borrowing is certainly one way of taking care of the tax bill. In fact, it is one of the three major ways to pay one's terminal taxes – but, it's not the best way. Let's say you borrowed a million dollars to pay the estate taxes; you would then have to pay back that million dollars with after-tax dollars. That means you would have to earn two million dollars, as well as pay the interest rate from the bank on that loan. If that rate is 10%, that's a $100,000 annual cost of the loan. Even if it's only 6%, that's still $60,000."

I saw Mr. Lindrum grimace. "Too much," he said.

2. Selling assets

Mr. Weirnicke spoke up, "Instead of borrowing, we'd sell one of our properties and raise the cash."

I was glad Mr. Weirnicke brought up the idea of selling properties. After I explained the problems involved in selling assets, I knew he would have to choose another option.

"You have to keep one thing in mind," I said, looking straight at Mr. Weirnicke. "The market always exists for the best assets. You might have a property in mind that you would like to sell, but what if there's no market for that particular property. You'd be forced to sell one of the properties that you'd rather keep. Let's take your west-end building and your east-end building as examples. Right now, as you've told me, your west-end building is your most lucrative property. But the east-end building is struggling a little. If you were to die tonight and had to raise the cash, do you think you'd be able to find a buyer for your east-end building? Certainly, there'd be buyers for the west-end property. Which would mean that your estate would be left with the struggling east-end property."

Mr. Weirnicke seemed a little stubborn on his point. "So, we'll sell one of our better properties. That's still better than buying life insurance now."

"Okay, let's say you sell your west-end property. You've said it's worth a million dollars. But why should I buy it for that?" I asked.

I saw Mr. Weirnicke straighten up in his chair. "Because it's worth a million dollars, that's why," he said exasperated.

"If it's worth a million dollars, I wouldn't buy it for that unless I thought it would be worth more than that tomorrow. Right?"

"Yes," he agreed somewhat grudgingly.

"Well, then, why would you sell a building to me and have your heirs forfeit the future growth of that asset, a property you spent many years building?"

Dying during a downturn

I watched as Mr. Weirnicke formulated another objection. At last he said, "What if that building is not worth that much when I die. The tax bill will be small and I will have wasted all my money on an insurance policy."

"Very good question," I said. "It's a real possibility. You've been around long enough to have personally seen the effects of real estate cycles. Ten years ago half of the downtown towers had see-through floors. But that's why you need insurance too – to protect you against such a downturn. When you build an estate like the one you're building, you put a lot of sweat equity in it. When there's a downturn, you may lose a lot of your equity in the properties, but your sweat equity is still there. Your family obviously benefits from the income your lucrative properties are generating now, but if those properties lose their value, your family will suffer. However, if you die during the wrong part of the business cycle and you have insurance, the policy will provide the cash flow your family was accustomed to when the property was earning money. You see, if you die when the properties are devalued, and have to sell them, your family would lose out on the value those properties would gain when the market swings upward again."

3. Insurance

Mr. Weirnicke and the rest of them fell silent, but Mrs. Weirnicke now spoke up. "What's the other way? You said there were three ways we could pay the tax bill."

"The third way to pay off a debt at death is through insurance. Using the power of insurance I can create a million dollars for you at 3% or 4% a year and you would never have to pay me more than 60 cents to create that dollar. Isn't paying 3% or 4% as a premium on a million-dollar life insurance contract better than paying 6% or 10% if you borrowed money. And when the million dollars from the life insurance comes in it's tax free.

"Plus, insurance will pay all your taxes and leave all your buildings in the family so that they, not someone else, can enjoy the future growth. Isn't that what you all have in mind when you are building your estates." I looked around at each of them. It was time to make my appeal to their conservative natures. "As developers you have all taken big chances, but you are not reckless. You've made an effort to claim your profits and build up a stronghold of equity. However, you haven't guarded yourselves against the one chance encounter that could unravel everything you've managed to build up. You certainly don't want to see it all wiped away by your deaths. I'm showing you the best way to protect yourselves."

When I was finished talking, Mr. Weirnicke glanced over at his wife, who nodded. He looked back at me, "Okay," he said, "if everyone else wants to go along with your option, I'll support it."

Everyone else did, and I sold my first and my sixth one-million-dollar policy in the same day.

Over the next few years I continued to sell to developers. In most cases I underpinned their debt as I had for Norm Howell. In other cases, I provided them with the solution to their tax liabilities. Although I sold a lot of insurance to developers, I also sold the same types of policies to other types of business owners who had similar debt and estate issues. In time, an extra zero became a permanent fixture on the policies I sold.

Growing with your clients

Over the last few chapters we've seen the importance of creative survival, of knowing your products, of passion, meeting the people and lastly of understanding your prospects. Understanding your prospects and clients, knowing their businesses, their risks and their psyches not only helps you to sell to them, but also ensures that you provide the right solutions to their problems. They feel they can rely on you for the right advice and will continue to do business with you in the future. The upside is that as your clients grow, their needs will become greater and your policies larger.

Throughout these chapters, you've seen a little bit about how I sell, but in Part III, I'd like to show you in greater depth the selling methods that I used to take me from a workaday agent selling to families and small business owners to a successful agent selling to top-notch professionals, wealthy business owners and wildly successful entrepreneurs. These selling strategies allowed me to sell to people who would not buy from any other agent. A former associate of mine once put it this way, "David," he said, "there are a number of people walking around today with insurance on their lives because you're in the business."

Three strategies for understanding your prospects

1) GET INSIDE YOUR PROSPECT'S PSYCHE.

2) LEARN YOUR PROSPECT'S BUSINESS.

3) UNDERSTAND YOUR PROSPECT'S RISKS.

PART III

How to sell megacases and
take your business to the top

If I am

properly prepared,

closing the case should be

a mere formality.

CHAPTER 7

Preparation: the Process Approach

As I began meeting wealthy prospects and making inroads into more lucrative markets, I quickly discovered the absolute necessity for preparation. I believe that I am able to close large and challenging deals because I know how to prepare for the case. I call my strategies for preparing a case the Process Approach, because I believe that most of the selling is done long before I make my presentation to the prospect. In fact, if I am properly prepared, closing the case should be a mere formality. It's not always that easy, and I'll be discussing my selling and closing strategies in the next chapter. For now, let me show you how I prepare for my cases.

The Process Approach I have developed involves 5 strategies for preparing a case: 1) Sell yourself. 2) Disarm your prospect. 3) Find the decision maker. 4) Find the loss. 5) Expose the loss. Before I take you through each of these strategies, I'd like to tell you something I always keep in mind during the preparation of a case – the 5 questions for evaluating a prospect.

The 5 questions for evaluating a prospect
1) *Will I do business with them?*
2) *Will they do business with me?*
3) *Do I realize their need?*
4) *Do they realize their need?*
5) *Can they pay the freight?*

If I can answer yes to these 5 questions, I know I have a prospect on my hands. And with the Process Approach, I can begin turning that prospect into a client.

Strategy 1: Sell yourself

The first strategy in the Process Approach, and the first thing I try to do when I am with a client, is sell myself. Selling myself means winning over the confidence of my prospect. I want him or her to trust that I will be able to offer the best possible solution to their problems. I do this by having confidence in myself – not arrogance, but the genuine confidence that comes from using all the strategies I have discussed so far in this book. I know my business and my products thoroughly, I am passionate about what I do, and I understand my prospects.

Selling myself to my prospect is especially critical when I am in competition with other agents, and in large cases I am never without heavy competition. I am often up against the prospect's current agent, or his or her relative. But I know that a prospect won't just hand their business over to their current agent or their relative unless they have confidence in their abilities.

The best agent with the worst company

A good example of how I sell myself to my prospects comes from an appointment I had fifteen years ago. An accountant I knew had suggested I see one of his wealthy clients, Phil Groyson, who was looking for $500,000 of insurance. Through shrewd management of a private portfolio of investments, Groyson had managed to turn a few million dollars into a few tens of millions. The accountant warned me that, aside from being shrewd, Phil was difficult to deal with.

I arrived at his office, a large uptown home which he had converted into his headquarters.

"Good afternoon, Mr. Groyson," I said as I was ushered into his office by his secretary.

Groyson sat behind a monstrous cherry wood desk. In reply to my greeting, he only grunted and motioned for me to sit in one of the armchairs across from his desk. I lowered myself into the soft leather seat, taking the opportunity to study his demeanor. He was obviously not the talkative type, and I would have to glean as much as possible through his expressions and body language. Although he was half-hidden behind his desk, I guessed that he was a shortish man. He had narrow shoulders, and a thin, gaunt face. The corners of his mouth were set in a permanent downturn, and his hair, thinning on top, was brushed back severely. His eyes were his most striking feature. They were small but brilliantly blue, and indicated a very sharp mind behind them.

"Mr. Groyson," I said at last, "I understand you are looking for $500,000 of insurance coverage."

"$250,000," he snapped.

"I'm sorry," I replied, "I was under the impression–"

"$250,000 on me, and $250,000 on my partner."

"I see," I said, "perhaps you could explain a little bit about your business and why you are looking for insurance."

"I'm a very private man, and I'd rather not get into my business affairs. Why don't you just give me a proposal for two $250,000 policies and I'll look at them."

At this point, I wondered why he had bothered to see me. If all he wanted from me was a quote, I could have done that over the phone. I knew there was more to this meeting than he was letting on. He was a busy man, and obviously not the type that enjoyed wasting time. I suspected he was putting me through some kind of test. I looked at his face and saw that he was staring in my direction – probing me for any sign of weakness.

I returned his unwavering gaze until his eyes wandered over to a two-foot-high stack of folders on the left side of his desk.

"Are those other insurance proposals?" I inquired.

"Yes," he replied with a near smile.

"If I provide you with another proposal will it go on top of that pile?" I asked.

He nodded silently.

"What good is a stack of proposals going to do you?"

"I'm going to take a look at them."

"You mean, you're going to assess those proposals?"

He nodded again.

"You can't do that," I declared.

"Pardon me," he replied.

"What will you be looking for?"

"The best company."

"I've got news for you," I replied. "You're better off with the best

agent with the worst company than with the worst agent with
the best company."

"Why is that?" he asked pointedly.

"Let's suppose," I began, "that I went out and got a proposal for
$15,000 of whole life from the ten top insurance companies. If you
look at it from my perspective, as an agent in the business, you know
that there are three things that impact on the premium. First, you have
the insurance company's investments – which are all made in the same
marketplace under the same government regulations. Second, you have
their administration costs – which don't differ much because there are
standards in the industry for things like salaries. And third, you have
the cost of the insurance – which is also very similar because they are
all working off similar mortality tables. If you bought a policy from any
one of these ten insurance companies there wouldn't be much difference
in price, perhaps a few percent difference here and there on things like
cash values and dividends. So you shouldn't be looking for which
company is the best, you should be looking for the best agent."

He leaned back in his chair and pondered over what I had said.
Obviously no other insurance agent had put it to him quite like that.
I knew I wouldn't stand much chance being lumped in with a
hundred other proposals. I had to sell myself, not my proposal.

At last, he said, "You're probably right." And then he fell silent
again. He certainly wasn't making this easy.

I broke the silence. "I gather you've purchased insurance before.
So what about that agent? Why do you want all these proposals?"

He straightened up in his chair. "Because I don't have a lot of
confidence in him."

"What company is he with?" I asked, and he told me the name.

"You know," I said, "that's one of the best companies in the country.
If you bought your two policies of $250,000 insurance through him,
you wouldn't be making any mistakes. So, you're really looking for the
best agent, not the best company. And if you want to work with me, I
can assure you that I'll certainly be representing one of the best companies.
The best agents tend to work with the best companies." I stopped for a
moment, and looked him straight in the eyes. He didn't blink and
neither did I. I continued, "Would you like me to be your agent?"

"I'll think about it," he said, again with a near smile.

I began to rise from my chair, "When you've thought it over

please give me a call and I'll put together my proposal for you. But I might make it for $100,000, or $1,000,000, instead of $250,000."

"Why would I need $1,000,000 of insurance?" he asked.

I lowered myself back into my chair. "I don't know," I replied. He gazed back blankly.

"I don't even know why you want $250,000 on you and your partner."

"We have a loan from the bank for $5,000,000. That's why," he said.

"So, you're buying this for the bank?"

"Yes. And I don't want whole life. I want term, because the loan is only for five years."

I still didn't understand how he came up with the $250,000 figure. How did that figure relate to the loan amount? I also didn't agree with his insistence on term insurance. I needed to ask him for more information. "Do you plan on paying off the $5,000,000 loan in five years?"

He nodded.

"If you do that," I said, "you'll have a $5,000,000 asset in five years. So why do you want term insurance? And why only $250,000 on each of you?"

He was silent again, this time his gaze wasn't fixed on me. It wandered slowly about the room. "I don't know," he replied. He seemed to actually enjoy his ignorance. It hit me that he was looking for someone with the confidence to challenge him. Anyone who could do that would certainly know their business and be able to service his needs.

"In five years when you have that $5,000,000 asset, you won't need insurance for your loan, but you will need insurance to take care of your estate taxes. So your need is permanent, not temporary. And you don't need $250,000 of insurance, you need $5,000,000 on both you and your partner."

He did ask me to be his agent, and I ended up insuring him and his partner for $5,000,000 each – of whole life, not term. Over the years I continued to sell both of them larger and larger amounts of insurance. Today, each holds over $25,000,000 of insurance with me and over $50,000,000 in term-certain annuities. So, it was well worth it for me to sell myself, rather than to get lost in the pile of proposals.

Strategy 2: Disarm your prospect

The next strategy I use in my Process Approach for preparing a case is disarming my prospect. When I disarm a prospect, I am opening them up so that they will give me the information I need. To disarm a client and get them to talk, I have to prove to them that I have their interests in mind, not mine. I go out of my way to tell my prospects that they may not even need me and that I don't need their business. Instead of seeing me as an adversary or someone out for himself, they begin to see me as someone who can help them achieve their goals. Let me show you what I mean by taking you through a case I worked on with another agent named Perry.

Perry, a young agent who had heard about my reputation as a closer of insurance megacases, called me one afternoon a few years ago to tell me he wanted my help on a very large and difficult case. We agreed to meet and discuss the case further.

During our meeting I learned a lot about Perry. He had been in the insurance business for seven years, selling medium-sized cases in the family and small business market. He was a solid agent whose average policy size was around the $300,000 mark, but he was eager to close a megacase. His wife's aunt was a tycoon in the real estate business, and he had known for a long time that she needed $10,000,000 of insurance. He dreamed about making the sale, but he wanted to wait until he had the experience and confidence to make an effective approach. He knew the aunt was not the type to give him the business because he was family – he would have to earn it. In fact, getting an appointment hadn't been easy, but he was persistent. He had been calling her for months and had only recently talked her into seeing him. That's when he called me. He wanted to bring me in to shore up his aunt's confidence in him, and to help clinch the deal.

The week after Perry and I met, we went to visit the aunt at her office, a large but modern and spartan room decorated in black and white. Perry and I sat on a couple of chairs waiting for his aunt to finish a phone call in another room. I turned around and noticed a massive abstract painting on the far wall. It was an all-white canvas with a splotch of black paint in the middle. I said to Perry, "Hey, do you think the person who spilled that black paint made it out of the office alive?"

"It's supposed to be there," he said. "It's called abstract art—" he stopped and turned away when he realized I was kidding.

"David," he said turning back to me, "do you remember what you're going to ask?" We had met an hour or so earlier and discussed the case. At this point Perry didn't know much, other than the fact that his aunt was supposed to be in the market for insurance as a way of financing her estate taxes. He knew she was wealthy, but the details of her wealth were not well-known. I had explained to Perry that I simply wanted to make this meeting a discovery of facts. Later, we would go away and draft a proposal. I watched Perry's knee go up and down rapidly. I nudged his leg with my shoe to steady him, "Perry, don't worry about a thing."

"She's not very tolerant—" Ingrid Isleman, Perry's aunt, walked in at that moment. I glanced at Perry as a red flush came over his face.

"Gentlemen," she said, as we rose to our feet. "That's all right," she continued, gesturing for us to resume our seated positions, as she took a seat behind her desk.

"Ms. Isleman," I said, "I understand you are looking for insurance."

"So I am told. My accountant says I need $10 million," she replied sternly, "but I'm not sure I agree with him." I saw Perry's leg begin to shake again.

"Ms. Isleman," I said, "I'm here today because Perry asked me to come along. I'm happy to be here, but I'm not here to sell you something you don't need. And I don't want the business unless I deserve it. I can tell you that I don't need it."

"Then why are you here?" she shot back sharply.

"I think I can explain—" Perry began nervously.

I nudged him again with my shoe and broke in, "I'm here as a resource for Perry. I have many years of experience with financing estate taxes through insurance, and perhaps my knowledge will be helpful. If you and Perry wish to discuss your estate matters with me, I am more than happy to oblige. You may develop confidence in my abilities, and maybe I'll earn your business, but I am not here to sell you something. At this point, I don't even know if you need insurance." Out of the corner of my eye I saw Perry bow his head.

"Fine," she said. "I have a large amount of equity tied up in properties. Properties that I want to pass on—" she glanced at Perry "— to my two daughters. My accountant estimates the estate tax will be $10 million."

We discussed her business affairs for a few more minutes. She talked quite enthusiastically about how she made her fortune buying run-down properties and converting them into highly successful luxury units. She had a Midas touch when it came to investing, and it was clear that she relished her talent. After a while, she said she had to be somewhere else in a few minutes. I thanked her for letting us see her and said we'd be in touch in the next few days with some kind of proposal.

As I drove Perry back to his office, he chastised me about my approach. "Why in the world would you suggest she doesn't need the insurance? If she begins to believe that then there'll be no case."

"She won't ever believe that," I replied. "She knows she needs the insurance. When I told her she might not need it, she realized that I had her interests in mind, not mine or yours, and that's when she began to talk."

Perry shook his head, "I guess so. But how can you be so sure."

"Because there will be estate taxes to pay."

"But why does she know she should do it with insurance?"

"Because she's smart, Perry. There are three ways to pay the tax bill: by borrowing against the assets, selling assets and through insurance. Insurance is the cheapest." For the next few minutes I explained in detail those three options which we explored in chapter 6 in the Lindrum, Weirnicke, and Bantam case. Perry was excited by our discussion; but his excitement would later turn out to jeopardize the case, which continued to be a struggle. I had to keep disarming the prospect and proving that I had her interests in mind. Because Perry was a relative, she was more suspicious of our motives than she otherwise would have been. She knew Perry didn't deal in her market and she wasn't prepared to hand him a winning lottery ticket.

The cool close

Perry and I prepared our proposal and I phoned Ingrid to tell her we were ready to come see her again. When I got her on the phone, she said, "You're too late. I'm sorry, but I've done the insurance with another agent."

"Have you written the check for the premium?" I asked.

"As a matter of fact, no," she said.

"Then can we still come and see you. If you're not happy with what we have to say, then that will be the end of it."

Begrudgingly she agreed to another meeting. When I got off the phone and explained to a rather anxious Perry that she had almost done the insurance with another agent, he became livid.

"You know why, David. It's because of what you said to her. She thinks you don't care about her business. All this stuff about her not needing insurance, and you not needing the business – she doesn't think you can do the job. You're too cavalier."

When he was finished, I replied, "Perry, your family connection is what she's concerned about. She's very suspicious of your motive. You're going to have to convince her that you're doing the business for her, and you have to behave like you're the person for the job. Stop acting desperate and nervous. That doesn't instill confidence."

"I hope you're right," he said with resignation.

A week later we went to see Ingrid and presented our proposal. After showing her our plan, she said she was pretty sure she was going to go ahead with the other agent's plan. "I do appreciate the time you've put into this proposal, David," she said, "but I've made up my mind."

"I understand," I replied, "and your decision is fine with me."

Perry began to fidget wildly. I tried to divert attention away from him, and asked her, "Before we go may I ask what it is you like about the plan you are going with."

The other plan was a whole life policy with a $100,000 premium to be paid for 10 years. The 10-year period was based on projected dividends which I felt were a little too optimistic. The plan we were showing was a stripped-down Universal Life policy with an initial premium of $98,000, and a guaranteed life-time cost of insurance of $80,000. From my point of view, she would be better off with our guaranteed premium than with the uncertain premium of the other plan. Our plan could only get better if interest was payable beyond the guaranteed floor rate of 4%, while the competitor's plan had a decent chance of getting worse. She was a very wise investor and I felt that she would suffer by losing the opportunity to invest the difference between the higher and lower premium.

"I like the fact that I stop paying premiums after 10 years," she replied.

"If it works out that way," I replied.

"What do you mean?" she asked.

"The plan you are going with is based on projections not guarantees. I can guarantee one thing about it, though. I can guarantee that how it turns out in reality will not be what you see on paper now."

Ingrid got up from her chair and wandered pensively over to the window. At that point, Perry nudged me and started whispering,

"David," he said in a desperate hush, "explain the three options the way you explained it to me in the car–"

I tried ignoring him. Whispering in front of a client is the surest way to destroy their trust. Once they see that, they know you have your own interests at heart, not theirs. Finally I got up to get away from him, and began pacing the room. But Perry didn't stop whispering.

"Perry," Ingrid blurted, "speak up so I can hear you too!"

Perry was too nervous to answer, and Ingrid shook her head in annoyance. She turned to me, "I will think about what you said, David."

Perry and I left her office and walked in silence until we got into my car. "David, I don't understand why you don't explain the three options. If you say she needs confidence in us, why don't you show her you know what you're talking about. So far, she hasn't seen a thing that proves you're an expert insurance agent."

"Perry," I replied, "I've told you she knows she needs the insurance. That's not why we're here. She simply wants to know what insurance plan and method of payment are best for her. That's what I'm trying to do – offer her the best insurance for her particular needs. I never bring up anything unless it's relevant."

Perry fell silent, and then later, close to his office, he asked, "David, is the deal blown?"

"I don't know," I replied. After Perry's antics, I thought our chances of getting the case were slim.

A few days later, I received a call from Ingrid. She wanted to know why I thought our proposal was the best. I told her she was an expert at saving and investing, otherwise she wouldn't have an insurance problem. I explained to her she should look for the most for the least. I thought she was better off paying a guaranteed lower rate for life and using the difference to make her own investments. She had a lot of cash flow from her properties and other investments. The last thing she needed was a savings plan. And the risk that she might be paying the higher premium for much longer than 10 years was real and made it a much less attractive proposal.

"You're right, David," she said, "that's how I see it myself." She paused for a moment. "David, why did you pursue this case after I told you I was going with the other agent?"

"Because I knew you weren't satisfied with the other agent's plan,"

I replied. "You would have written the check otherwise. I never give up on a case when I know that I can still be of assistance. I knew that if I could get inside your head and figure out why you weren't satisfied, I would be able to help you."

Ingrid decided to go ahead with our proposal for $10 million of insurance and her nephew closed his first megacase.

Disarming the prospect is crucial, because they must trust you enough to talk. If they don't talk, you aren't going to get the information you need to fully prepare a case and ultimately sell it. The next two strategies – find the decision maker and find the loss – depend on the prospect opening up and offering you vital information.

Strategy 3: Find the decision maker

Early in my career I made the mistake of presenting proposals to people who weren't the decision makers. I quickly learned that this was an absolute waste of my time. If I wasn't talking to the decision maker, the person who would be writing the check, I wasn't talking to a prospect. So, find the decision maker became strategy 3 in my Process Approach.

I developed the discipline of finding the decision maker when I worked in the small-business market. Sometime in my first year in the business I met Clyde, who owned a clothing store. I got an appointment to see him one evening at his store after hours. We sat in the bookkeeper's small office.

"Clyde," I began, "I'd like to discuss some ways of protecting your family in the event of your death."

"By all means, David. I'm a real believer in insurance. My father died without insurance when I was young and it was pretty horrible."

Clyde was an obvious supporter of insurance, and a sale seemed a likely conclusion to our meeting, but I needed to know more about Clyde's business and family situation. He was an exceptionally easy-going guy, so it wasn't hard to establish a rapport and get him to talk, but the more we talked, the more concerned I became. He began telling me more about his wife and I started thinking that I was talking to the wrong person. In telling me about his business, Clyde revealed that he didn't make a move without the consent of his wife. The decision to open the store at this location was hers, and she made most of the buying decisions.

"Clyde," I asked, "why don't I come see you and your wife next week and we can sit down together and discuss the insurance."

"Um," he mumbled, "I think we can talk about it tonight and I'll explain it to her."

"Clyde, if I show you an insurance plan tonight that you like, will you buy it tonight?"

"Well, I would have to speak to my wife about it, of course."

"I understand. It's only fair that she's part of the discussion. That's why I'd like to see her."

"But I can explain it to her myself."

"It's taken me months to learn all about the policy I'd like to show you, I'd hardly expect you to learn it well enough in one night to explain to somebody else."

"But isn't it simple?"

"The point is, what will you do if she says she doesn't like something about the policy."

"I guess she wouldn't buy it."

"But if I was there, I'd be able to answer her objections, I'd be able to show her we can do something the way she wants it and still make sure you're insured. In fairness to her, I should sit down with her and discuss it."

He fell silent.

"Listen," I said, "I don't expect you to sell your wife insurance, that's my job. And you've already said how important insurance is to you, you don't really want to go much longer without it, do you?"

"I guess not. I'll call her now," he replied.

The following week I met Clyde and his wife, and after a couple of hours of addressing her objections, she finally agreed to let her husband buy the insurance. I saw the relief on Clyde's face when she gave him the go-ahead.

Finding the decision maker is just as crucial in large business cases. You may be excited to have an appointment with a vice-president, or even the CEO, but still, you might not be meeting with the person who can make the ultimate decision. Whenever I meet with a potential prospect, I set myself the goal of finding out by the end of that meeting whether or not they are the decision maker. If it turns out that someone else is, I will only come back for a second meeting if that person is present. In Chapter 9, I'll tell you about a giant globe-trotting case I worked on where finding the decision maker proved to be a wild goose chase.

Strategy 4: Find the loss

My next strategy in the Process Approach is to find the loss. I owe this bit of wisdom to Isaac Kilbrick who is known as the father of business insurance. I met him when I was a young agent about 30 years ago at a conference. After he spoke, I walked up to him and asked him what the secret of selling business insurance was. He looked me straight in the eyes and replied, "Look for the loss." And that's what I began to do.

Finding the loss means uncovering a weak point – the Achilles Heel – that can be protected by insurance. If you can find the loss, you have a case. Your prospect needs you. So, getting the information you need and then being able to zero in on the loss quickly and accurately is essential to securing business cases. In chapter 6, I showed you how I approached developers by asking them how many times they signed for the loan. That one simple question often unearthed the loss for me, and led to large insurance sales.

I sell time

The loss that I am interested in is the kind that depends on a person's time. Once someone borrows money and puts it to use, the only way out depends on them having enough time to pay off the loan. So, in essence, that is what I sell – time. Time in the form of money. I sell the money that would have been made if the insured had lived.

Thinking of insurance this way helps me hone in on the loss. The second signature is only one example of a loss that depends on a person's time. I find many losses in the form of key people. A key person might be the owner or he or she might be someone the owner had hired. When I look at a company, I see it as a three-legged stool. The first leg represents capital, the second leg represents labor, and the third leg management. Key people are found in that third leg, because it is what management does with the first two legs that makes a business successful. You'll find that key people are responsible for various things, such as: return on investment capital; making sure physical plants, equipment and workers are working efficiently; ensuring inventories are converted into sales; the timely collection of accounts receivable; creating intellectual property; establishing goodwill and customer loyalty.

The three exits

If the key people don't have enough time to fulfill their responsibilities, the company will suffer. There are two major ways a company can lose the time of its key people: one, they could die or get sick; and two, they could quit. There's a third possible loss of time, but this affects the key person rather than the company. The company could fire him or her. In other words a key person has three possible exits: 1) they can get carried out, 2) they can walk out of their own accord, or 3) they can get pushed out. All three losses interest me because insurance can protect against all of them.

Strategy 5: Expose the loss

Once I have found the loss, the company's weak spot, my next strategy in the Process Approach is to expose it. Let me show you two interesting cases I worked on where finding the loss and exposing it were instrumental in getting the sale.

Louis Harvey's most important asset

Louis Harvey owned a highly successful software company. He was the CEO, but the company was really run by the vice-president. Louis was looking to raise capital for the company and wanted to get in touch with the investment arm of an insurer I had a close relationship with. A mutual friend arranged for Louis and I to meet and discuss how I could introduce him to the insurance company.

I seized the opportunity to get involved. In the process, I would gain an incredible amount of information about Louis and his company, which I would eventually use to approach him about insurance. After a few months of faxes, letters from lawyers and accountants on both sides, and many conference calls, Louis, his entourage and I flew out to visit the headquarters of the insurance company. The meeting went well and Louis, who was normally cantankerous, displayed obvious excitement and gratitude. We sat beside each other on his jet to fly back to Toronto, and I listened to him expound upon the vision for his corporate empire. He saw his company growing from a $50 million concern to over $200 million within two years.

In celebration of the event, Boris, the vice-president, uncorked a bottle of champagne and went through the aisle pouring a drink for everyone. Boris, a software engineer, was the brains behind the operation. He was a highly creative programmer who designed and developed every program the company marketed. When Boris got to our seat, Louis turned to me and said, "This is Boris – my key man."

"Then why haven't we insured him?" I asked immediately.

The excitement he'd displayed all day fell instantly from his face. "I don't need any god-damned insurance on Boris."

My reply to this statement was in my mouth even before I was conscious of it, and it erupted uncensored. "Don't B.S. me, Louis. If you don't have a key man worth insuring, you don't have a key man."

Louis shot me an indignant look and turned away. I gathered that people didn't speak to Louis that way. A wall of silence came down between our seats. He sipped his champagne and busied himself with discussions across the aisle. Not a word was spoken between us for the rest of the flight. I stared out the window for the longest time, gazing at the clouds below and wondering if I had blown my chances. I concluded that Louis might not forgive my directness, but that at least I had told him the truth. When the jet landed, we disembarked in silence and entered our respective limousines, without even a hint at a good-bye.

As it happened, I ran into Louis on the street a week later. He had recaptured his excitement from the previous week and seemed to forget our little tiff.

"David," he said as he reached his hand out to shake mine, "how are you?"

"Great, you?" I replied.

"Wonderful. The last little loose-ends are being wrapped up today. You know that key man insurance you were talking about. Well, I did think about it, and actually brought it up with my accountants, and we all agreed we don't need it."

I could tell by the way he said this that he wanted to know more about how I felt about his decision. He might have been temperamental, but he was shrewd. He wanted to make certain he was doing the right thing. We walked together down the block and I offered my opinion.

"Louis," I said, "you have a company which depends upon the highly specialized knowledge of your vice-president, Boris. I have studied the balance sheets, and last year it had sales in excess of $10 million and net profits of more than $1 million. If Boris were to die, you would lose all his specialized knowledge, and the company would suffer dearly. Surely you don't want to have to step in and run Boris's highly specialized company, even if you had his knowledge. I gather that your accountants are looking at insurance premiums for Boris as an unnecessary expense. They'd rather you spend the money on the business. But if Boris isn't around, there won't be any business."

He nodded and we walked further. I sensed him coming around to the idea that he couldn't do without Boris. He was not, however, coming round to the idea that insurance was the best solution to his problem. Convincing Louis to buy the insurance was no easy task, and I'd like to show you how I managed to do so in the next chapter on the sales meeting. Right now, I'd like to discuss the next step in the selling process: present the solution.

Presenting the solution

Once I have found and exposed the loss, I then present my insurance solution as the best way to protect against the loss. In fact, I never expose the loss, until I have figured out the solution. Presenting the solution is the end result of all my preparation, and the bridge between the Process Approach for preparing the case and the sales meeting. I'd like to end this chapter with another key-person story and take you through how I found the loss, exposed it and then presented my insurance solution.

What if Robert walks across the street?

Joel owned a large chain of record stores across the country. He was the CEO, but relied heavily on the expertise of one his employees, Robert, who was especially talented at finding new store locations. Because the company was putting all of its efforts into expansion in order to seize market share, Robert's role was vital to the bottom line. Without Robert, the company would surely suffer. Joel, who had heard of me through an acquaintance, called me to buy insurance on Robert. Joel wanted to protect against Robert's untimely death, and was thus already sold on the concept of key-person insurance. The solution he wanted from me was term insurance. I asked to see him in person to discuss the matter further and he agreed.

We met at his office the next day and discussed at length how he operated his business, and exactly where Robert fit in. Unfortunately, after exploring a little deeper, I found I didn't agree with Joel about what his loss was. I decided to turn the subject back to insurance.

"Joel," I said, "Robert is 55 years old and plans to retire in five years, and you want to insure him for those five years. And that's why you want term insurance. Is that correct?"

"Yes," he replied.

"In my business, Joel," I said, "I'm trained to look for the loss, and I don't believe that Robert's death is your real loss. This may be an unlikely stance for an insurance agent, but I have my reasons. Robert is key to your operations – without him your plans for expansion would suffer. He knows the business inside-out, and training someone to replace him would take time – that's why his death would affect you. But I think a greater loss, which is being overlooked, would occur if Robert took his in-depth knowledge of your business across the street to one of your competitors." I watched as Joel's eyes widened. "And what if, after he left, he came back on a raiding mission to build up his new expansion team. Working with people he knows would certainly make his new position easier. So you'd probably end up losing more than just Robert's expertise."

"So how am I supposed to make sure he doesn't leave."

"The kind of insurance I sell insures against that possibility as well. First, let me develop a package that will protect you against his death. And I'll add a disability waiver to protect you against his becoming ill. And then let me build in a component so that Robert won't be susceptible to the blandishments of one of your competitors."

"How will you do that?" Joel asked.

"By putting golden handcuffs on him."

I explained to Joel that if we put an insurance plan with a high cash value on Robert's life, he would be encouraged to stay with Joel in order to benefit from the savings when he came to retire. Leaving would mean forfeiting the cash value – the golden handcuffs. Or, I told Joel, if he wanted to terminate Robert at some time, he could offer the cash value as a severance package – the golden handshake. And if Robert stayed until retiring, he could take the cash value for himself – the golden parachute. So, with this one policy we would be covering the three possible losses I mentioned earlier. Robert might walk out on his own accord, get pushed out, or get carried out. For each contingency, the insurance plan was there as protection.

My most valuable asset

Preparation is the part of the sales process that comes before I present my proposal. If a case is not properly prepared I know I am in serious danger of losing it somewhere along the way. Early in my career I lost some large cases after months of working on them, because I didn't prepare properly from the beginning. I am extra careful now to ensure that I am fully prepared and protect myself as much as possible against losing my most valuable asset – my time. But if I have used the Process Approach to prepare my case, I feel confident that I am close to turning my prospect into a client.

The process approach: 5 strategies for preparing cases

1) SELL YOURSELF.

2) DISARM YOUR PROSPECT.

3) FIND THE DECISION MAKER.

4) FIND THE LOSS.

5) EXPOSE THE LOSS.

If I ask

you for the time,

don't build me

a watch.

CHAPTER 8

*The sales meeting: turning
prospects into clients*

K nowing how to prepare for a case is obviously a
key to success in our business, but we don't get
paid for that part. Our income depends on selling
the solution to the prospect. Selling is a little like
horse racing – you can bet on the best horse, but if
she doesn't perform on the day of the race, you'll lose. The same
goes for us – no matter how wonderful our solution, the close
depends on our behavior in the sales meeting. For this reason, I
have developed the following 4 strategies to make sure I perform
well enough to turn the prospect into a client: 1) Sell the
benefits, not the features. 2) Confront each objection head on.
3) Reveal the logic of your solution. 4) Ask for the premium.

Strategy 1: Sell the benefit, not the features

People don't buy insurance because they like the features or the
mechanics of a plan. They buy insurance because it benefits them –
it meets a need. That's why I sell the benefits. Selling the benefits is
crucial to all types of selling. In fact, I learned this strategy, not while
selling insurance, but during my former career as a paint salesman.
Because it highlights so well the necessity of selling the benefits, I'd
like to take you back in time to one of my first ever sales meetings.

Learning to sell the benefits

It was the summer of 1957 and I was a neophyte salesman for McInley & McDougall. I was excited to have landed an opportunity to see Mr. Norwell and his wife. I had been trying for weeks to get an appointment with them because, although they were small, they were one of the most successful painting companies in the city. They did a lot of contract work on the new buildings that were sprouting up in the downtown core and I'd heard through my network that they'd been tremendously busy lately.

On the afternoon of our meeting, I met Mr. and Mrs. Norwell in their small boardroom. He was a tall, older man, with thinning gray hair. She was the same age but smaller and more dynamic. After the opening pleasantries were out of the way, I began my well-rehearsed pitch. "The company that manufactures our paint is one of the largest in North America, and their plant is the most technologically up-to-date. In fact, their instruments are so impeccably precise they guarantee quality levels far higher than any of their competitors...."

As I ran through all of the many, genuinely good features of the paint, I began to notice that something was wrong. At what I considered to be a key moment in my spiel, I paused dramatically and turned to face Mr. Norwell. I wanted to catch his eye and establish a personal connection. But when I looked at him, I saw a smooth, reflecting pond. Panicking, I turned desperately to look at his wife. She had the same empty expression. I had put them both to sleep.

I felt awful. But who could blame them – I'd be half asleep too if I had to listen to my drivel. The Norwells didn't care about the paint company and its plant. They didn't even care about the paint. But what did they care about? The answer soon hit me – the Norwells used paint for the benefits it gave them. As a former interior decorator, I knew that people bought paint for three possible reasons: decoration, sanitation and preservation. Mr. and Mrs. Norwell would buy paint from me for one, two, or all three of those reasons. I decided on my new angle – I would sell the Norwells the benefits of paint.

I turned to Mrs. Norwell, the more creative and sensitive of the two. "Mrs. Norwell," I said, "let me show you what this paint does." I brought out a sample can that I carried, popped open the lid, took a small brush and a small square piece of white board out from my briefcase. I brushed a little paint on the surface of the white board. I did it delicately, gently, and held the board at an angle so the afternoon sunlight coming through the window played sweetly over the dewy layer of fresh paint. "Look there, Mrs. Norwell," I said. "Look at that! Isn't that incredible, that glow. No other paint glows like that. When people sit in a room where the walls are painted like this, they feel something, there is a joy." I looked at her face, the corners of her lips turned up and there was life in her eyes.

I turned to her husband. "Mr. Norwell, this paint you see will keep its luster, not just for a few minutes, but for a few years. But more than that, it will protect the walls it's painted on. Years later the walls will look freshly painted, no peeling or cracking, and the surface will always be smooth, easy to clean...." I saw Mr. Norwell nod slightly.

Now I had their attention. I could see them both imagining their walls and their clients' walls painted with my paint. Quietly, deftly, I put down the sample on the desk in front of Mrs. Norwell. Her eyes followed the little splotch of paint. I reached into my briefcase for my order pad and held my pen poised above it. In a near whisper I said, "Would you like the paint to be delivered next Tuesday or next Thursday?"

There was a moment of silence. I waited patiently. Inside I was trembling, with excitement, nervousness. I saw Mr. Norwell's lips move, "Tuesday's fine."

Don't build me a watch

I continued to focus on the benefits of paint and made many other large paint sales. Later, when I was in the insurance business, I was reminded to sell the benefits, not the features, by a prospect who happened to be one of the wealthiest men in the country. He had asked me a question, and I launched into an elaborate dissection of the mechanics of the policy. He soon interrupted me and said, "David, if I ask you for the time, don't build me a watch." I realized then the necessity of zeroing in on the benefits of insurance instead of on the insurance policy. Expounding upon the policy features, or delving into the mechanics of the plan only distracts prospects. By selling the benefits you highlight your prospect's need for insurance, and show them why insurance is their best solution. No matter what size the case, or how complicated it might be, I still focus on the power of insurance – rather than the premium for insurance – to provide for my prospect's family after their death. I sell the benefits.

Strategy 2: Confront each objection head on

Selling the benefits will help you stay on track, but it won't mean a cakewalk to the close. You'll still have to weather the inevitable storm of objections. How you handle those objections can mean the difference between a sale and no sale. If you try to evade the objection, or sell around it, you'll show the prospect that you are no longer in control; and when that happens, they'll lose confidence in you and you'll lose the case. But if you confront each objection head on, you'll find your way to the close. I have discovered three approaches that help me confront objections head on.

Approach 1: I passionately believe in my product
I have delivered too many death claims, have saved too many families from financial ruin, to let a prospect's objection shake my faith in my product. They can object all they want, but I am a rock when it comes to insurance. My job is to answer their objections and make them a believer.

Approach 2: I prepare the prospect's case for not buying insurance better than they can
In the previous chapter, I showed you strategies for preparing the case for buying insurance. But it is just as important to prepare the case for not buying the insurance, and you must do that better than the prospect. As Louis Nizer, in his book *My Life In Court*, wrote, "Preparation will make the dull man appear bright, and the bright man appear brilliant." This helps you anticipate all the possible objections and develop responses to them, so you won't be caught off guard in the sales meeting.

Approach 3: I know objections are buying signals
I love objections. I love them because I know they are buying signals. I am always surprised that some agents don't like objections. In fact, a couple of months ago, I was talking to a young agent named Harold who complained to me that he couldn't get a prospect to buy because the prospect had too many objections. I told Harold that his problem

was he didn't realize that the objections he was hearing were really pleas to buy.

"I don't understand," Harold had said to me.

"Harold," I replied to him, "imagine a young couple shopping for a home. They come across a house they seem to like, but when the real-estate agent asks them how they feel about it, the wife says, 'Well, I don't like the tiling.'" I looked Harold in the eye. "What do you think has just happened?"

"Sounds like she doesn't want to buy the house."

"Exactly the opposite," I declared.

"But I don't get it. To me it sounds like she doesn't want it and the tile thing is an excuse."

"Harold, if she didn't want the house, she would have just left with her husband. But she does want the house, she just wishes it had different tiling."

"Oh," Harold said.

"So now what do you do?" I asked him.

"I don't know. What would you do?"

"If it was me, I would ask her if there was anything else she didn't like about the house. She might bring up a couple of other things – the fact that there's no garden, the basement's not finished. Then I would ask her if all those things were fixed would she buy the house. When she says yes, all I have to do is deal with her objections – that might mean making renovations or lowering the price of the house, but when we're through, I'd have sold the house." I saw Harold nod. "And it's the same in the insurance business. When a prospect objects, they are saying to you that they like what you are showing them only they don't like some particular aspect, or maybe it's a lot of particular aspects. Still, if you can answer each of the objections, you will get the close."

Harold continued to quiz me about objections. "But how do you answer those objections?" Harold asked.

"It depends on the objection. Sometimes it's as simple as making a modification to your proposal. If the prospect says she doesn't want to pay premiums for the rest of her life, all you have to do is show her a plan that pays up in ten or fifteen years."

"But I'm not talking about those kinds of objections. Those are easy. I know how to deal with them. The ones that get me are the ones where the prospect just doesn't believe in insurance. It's like they've put up a brick wall."

"Well, those are easy too, Harold," I said, somewhat facetiously.

"How?" he asked, glaring at me.

"Simple – reveal the logic of your solution."

Strategy 3: Reveal the logic of your solution

As Harold intimated, it's no problem dealing with easy objections head on – even Harold knows how to do that. The tough ones, though, are another thing altogether. Over the years, I have come across some extremely difficult objections that I have solved only by creating new ways of doing things, and I will show you some examples in the next chapter. But these exceptions aside, tough objections of the type Harold was referring to can be overcome by revealing the logic of your solution. Harold was right – tough objections stem from a prospect's prejudice against insurance. To some people, insurance isn't the beautiful word it is to us. To them it means a waste of money, or even a racket. But that's because they don't know insurance they way we do; they don't understand what it can do for them. But you still have to confront their tough objections head on. The way to do that is by revealing the logic of our solutions; that's how you break through their prejudice. For this strategy, I usually use one of three tools: analogies, numbers, or words.

Tool 1: Analogies

Throughout the book, you have seen me use analogies many times, like the time I compared the doctor to a money machine in his basement, or the time I compared buying insurance to saving a prospect's family from a fire in a movie theater. Here are a couple of other cases where analogies helped me tear down a prospect's prejudice.

Take the elevator to the penthouse

In the early years of my career I had an appointment with a young doctor. Within a few minutes, it was obvious that he had made up his mind – insurance was something he would never need. He made a lot of money, and was proud of his ability to save. He bragged to me that he would one day have a million dollars. I had told him that he should protect his income for his family through insurance, but he simply didn't want to spend the money. He liked having his money where he could see it. Paying premiums would only detract from the money he would be able to save. Clearly he didn't understand what I was proposing to him. He loved his savings bonds, his mutual funds, his stock portfolio, his term accounts. He had taken advantage of nearly every financial instrument, except one. I needed a way to break through his prejudice and reveal to him the most amazing savings plan ever.

Close to the end of our meeting, I decided to take another run at him. I said, "Your goal is to accumulate $1,000,000. That's certainly an admirable goal. Anyone with that kind of money would have no trouble supporting themselves and their family and never have to work again. But let's say that your $1,000,000 is represented by the penthouse apartment in a 32-story building. If your goal is to get there, how would you do it? Would you take the stairs, or the elevator?" It was obviously a rhetorical question – and he had no intention of answering it – so he was shocked when I said, "Obviously, you're the type of person that would take the stairs."

"Pardon me," he said somewhat exasperated.

"That's what you're doing now. You're taking the stairs to your $1,000,000, instead of the elevator."

He glared at me, waiting for me to explain.

"When you save money in the types of plans you're using, you are taking the stairs. When you invest in high-yield stocks, you might be taking three steps at a time, instead of two, but you're still taking the stairs. The problem about taking the stairs is that you can get stuck there. Say you break a leg, or trip and kill yourself – you won't be getting any higher. And if you haven't been climbing the stairs long enough to reach the penthouse, you'll be stuck where you are, and that might be the second floor or the twenty-second floor. In any case, you'll never achieve your goal. So where does that put you and your family?" I paused and looked at him, but he remained silent.

"But," I continued, "with insurance, you won't get stuck. With the waiver of premium, if you get injured, I will press the elevator button for you one floor at a time until you reach the penthouse. If you die, I'll press the express button and take you straight to the penthouse."

The doctor nodded. A few minutes later I left his office with a premium check in my hand. My simple story of the penthouse and the elevator revealed the logic of my plan.

Not buying insurance is like leaving your wife

Back in the '60s I had an appointment with a newlywed couple. The husband sat beside his shy new wife on their living room sofa and talked with pride about his sense of family and his conservative background. He aspired to emulate his father whom he regarded as a staunch caretaker and loyal husband to his mother, who was a traditional homemaker. But his father never had insurance, and so he didn't see the reason for having it either. As a new husband, his priority was to furnish their new house, and he didn't want to waste money on insurance when he could be spending it on a new dining-room table. I knew that in order to show him the logic of insurance, I would have to speak his language. So I made my appeal to his sense of family loyalty.

"Look," I said, "you've taken your wife away from a perfectly good home where her father was happy to support her. By asking for her hand in marriage and promising to look after her, you have replaced her father's commitment. When you die, if you don't have adequate life insurance, you're really going to abscond."

When I finished speaking, I saw him glance downward and ponder. After a while, he took his wife's hand, looked up at me and said, "I'll do anything to take care of my wife, Mr. Cowper."

Suddenly insurance seemed much more important to him than a love-seat or new television. It was a responsibility he had to his wife and their family. I pulled out my application, handed him a pen, and watched him sign.

Tool 2: Numbers

Analogies are wonderfully effective tools, but sometimes all it takes is numbers. You may remember the case of Louis Harvey and his key man Boris from the last chapter. Louis was a hard nut to crack. I had managed to convince him that losing Boris would drastically hurt his business, and I had shown him how insurance could protect against that loss, but Louis had a deep prejudice against insurance and still didn't see the value in my plan. I knew that Louis was a very logical person who loved his numbers and his money. In order to get him to buy, I would have to discuss my plan in terms he was familiar with.

Changing the identity of your asset

During one of our encounters, Louis said to me, "David, I have faith in you and I'm sure Boris is worth every penny of the policy you're asking me to purchase on him, but I just can't justify it right now. Our company is in a high-growth phase. Boris himself would be the first to tell you that we need to spend every thin dime we have on getting new products to market before our competition beats us to it. If we don't, we'll be frozen out of key markets. I just can't take money out of the company for insurance premiums right now."

"You make it sound like premiums are an expense. Like it's money you're spending just in case Boris dies."

"Well, that's what they are, right?"

"Louis, you have cash reserves in your company bank accounts, don't you?"

"Sure," he replied, "but we use some of those for paying some of our taxes and other irregular expenses. I can't spare the amount you're asking for."

"I'm sure you can't. And I'm not asking you to. The way I look at it, you can do one of two things. One, leave the money in your corporate bank account where you access it if you need to, or, two, transfer it to another account created for insurance. In the second case, some of the money will go toward the cost of insurance, but the rest will grow as a cash value. All you will have done is change the identity of the cash asset, from cash in the bank to cash value in the policy. With the insurance account, the company will be protected against the damage that Boris's death would cause. And if you need the money, you can borrow against the cash value."

"Yeah, that sounds great, sure," he said, "but what would it cost?"

"Well, what if we look at two years of your company's gross sales – how much is that?"

"$20,000,000."

"Okay then, let me show you how little it would take to insure that amount. One percent of two years sales would be $200,000. Ten percent of that $200,000 would be $20,000. That's only one-tenth of one percent of your annual gross sales. What if I could insure you for two full years of sales for that amount? Would you say that's a good deal?"

"Well, that looks good but I'm still skeptical, David," he said.

"How about if your vice-president dies and I inject $2,000,000 tax-free into your company? That's the equivalent of a 10% after-tax profit on $20,000,000 in sales – guaranteed."

"Hmmm...."

"Let me put it another way. If your taxes or cost of doing business went up by one-tenth of one percent of sales would you be out of business tomorrow?"

"No, of course not."

"Would you have to change any of your corporate strategies? Would fewer products make it to market? Would they be distributed or marketed less effectively?"

"Well, no."

"So, the premium is affordable. You can find the money in your current cash assets, and the cash will still be available to you as the cash value of the policy after you pay the premiums. All you'll really be doing is changing the identity of that cash asset and, in the process of that change, you'll be picking up $2,000,000 in insurance so that if Boris dies, you'll not only have the cash you started with, but $2,000,000 to offset the next two years profits."

When I left that short meeting I had another $2 million dollars in whole life insurance on the books. Louis became so convinced about the concept of key person insurance that we ended up placing over $6 million of life insurance on various key people in his company.

Whenever I manage to reach a close by revealing the logic of my numbers I am reminded of Pythagoras, the famous Greek mathematician, who said, "Numbers have a way of taking a man by the hand and gently leading him down the path of reason."

Tool 3: Words

Analogies and numbers – both are great tools for revealing the logic of your plan. But sometimes, you need little more than a few words, a mere phrase, to get your prospect to see the light. As salespeople, words are our most basic, and most important tool. To achieve greatness in our business we must become masters of words. I don't collect stamps or coins, but I do collect words and phrases. I pinch them from others, bastardize common sayings, and invent new ones myself. And I stockpile them all in a mental arsenal. After over thirty

years in sales, I have a phrase for virtually every sales situation.
To the people I work with, the many phrases I use are known as
Cowperisms. The label makes me a little uncomfortable because I
certainly don't deserve credit for coining them all. If I deserve any
credit, it's for spreading them around so much. The following story
will show you how powerful one of those simple phrases can be.

The $2 million-dollar mistake

Late in the afternoon on a Friday in April, I was at my desk trying to
iron out the finer points of an upcoming case, when my phone rang.
I said hello and was pleased to hear it was one of my clients, Dominic
Gregory, calling from London England. He had moved across the
Atlantic two years ago and, although we spoke only occasionally, I was
always happy to chat with him – especially since he was insured for
$2 million dollars in a 5-year-term policy which would soon be coming
up for renewal. I was hoping to get him to convert to whole life.

"David," he started, after exchanging quick hellos, "I have this
letter on my desk from the insurance company – they're asking for
$20,000."

"So send them the check," I replied.

"Well, it just seems so high, David," he replied. "I only paid
$12,000 last year and $20,000 seems very steep for a half-million
dollar policy."

"Dominic, your policy is for $2 million," I replied, "and your
premiums are going up because you have term insurance. I told
you five years ago that this would happen. You need the insurance,
and it's time we converted it."

"Well, I don't know about that. I can't even remember why I
have the insurance. I probably don't need it. And I'm certainly not
thrilled about throwing away $20,000," he said, in exasperation.

"Dominic," I replied calmly, "when are you going to be
in Canada next?"

"August, I think."

"Good, why don't we get together then. We'll look at your entire
insurance portfolio and you can make a proper decision then about
what to do with the policy."

"But what about this premium? If I don't pay by the end of the
week, it will lapse and I'm really not comfortable with the amount."

I sensed that Dominic was prepared to walk away from the policy. The benefit of having the insurance in force was obviously invisible to him. All he saw was the cost. I had to find a way to get him to pay the premium. I did a quick mental search for the right phrase. Within a few seconds, I had it – one that I had used many times before. "Dominic," I said, "when this conversation is finished and you hang up the phone, you are going to make a mistake. You are either going to make a $20,000 mistake, or a $2,000,000 mistake. Either way it will be a mistake."

That did it. There was silence on the other end of the line for what seemed like ages before he said, in a soft, resigned voice, "Well, okay. When you put it like that, I guess I'd better wire the money and then we should definitely get together in August to sort this out."

The premium was paid on time and we did meet in August. Not only did I avoid a lapse, but I was also able to convert that $20,000 annual term premium to a $65,000 permanent-plan premium.

OTHER COWPERISMS
Here are some of my favorite phrases and how I use them.

Tax-free dollars
When faced with a prospect who objected to paying her estate taxes through insurance, I said, "There are only two kinds of dollars: taxable and tax-free – not enough tax-free and too many taxable dollars." I wanted her to view insurance, with its tax-free death benefit, not as an enemy, but as her ally in her war against taxes.

A permanent problem
When faced with a prospect who insists on term insurance when whole-life is what they need, I'll point out that, "You cannot solve a permanent problem with a temporary solution."

Who owns your estate?
The simple question, "Have you ever figured out what part of your estate does not belong to you?" is a powerful reminder that we are ultimately in partnership with the government.

Permanent income
I used to sell a lot of disability insurance with the following simple phrase: "Your challenge, Mr. Prospect, is how do you move from temporary income to permanent income."

Retirement planning

To a prospect who takes advantage of their retirement savings privileges, I say, "The largest loophole in your plan to retire is the chance that your annual deposits won't be made because your earning power is interrupted or destroyed by sickness or disability."

Bringing work home

In the Norm Howell case I discussed in chapter 6, I showed you a phrase that, over the years, has opened and closed nearly every business case for me. In order to finance a small strip mall, Norm had gone to the bank for a $900,000 loan. He hadn't realized the risk he had taken until I said, "Norm, how many times did you sign for the bank loan?" As is common for private businesses, Norm had signed personally, exposing his family to the pillaging of creditors should he die with the debt outstanding.

Dying before your time

When prospects like Norm Howell say to me that their debt situation is temporary and they'll have all their loans cleared by the time they complete their project, I point out that, "No one dies at the beginning of something or at the end of something, but usually in the middle of something."

Underpinning debt

The cornerstone of my approach to underpinning debt is summed up in the phrase, "A debt should never last longer than the person that created it." I use it when prospects have trouble seeing that their entrepreneurship puts not only themselves at risk, but also their heirs.

Insurance costs too much

When a prospect complains that the insurance costs too much, I reply, "It isn't the insurance that costs too much; it's the groceries, the car payments, the mortgage, the gas bill, the phone bill, the cable bill. If you're having trouble paying for those costs now, while you have an income, imagine how you would cope without an income."

The Gulf War

Some very effective phrases are adaptations from current phrases used by the media. During the Gulf War, reporters and writers began tossing around the words 'escalating' and 'de-escalating' when referring to tensions and violence in the Middle East. I decided to adopt the words myself, and began referring to 'escalating' and 'de-escalating' premiums when trying to show a prospect the difference between term and whole life. I was able to clearly communicate my point, because the words resonated with the prospect. De-escalation was a good thing – both in war and for insurance policies.

Strategy 4: Ask for the premium

After you've confronted all of your prospect's objections head on and satisfied them that your solution is their only choice, the case is closed – or almost. You've got one more thing left to do – ask for the premium. It should be a formality, and it is, but asking for a check for $10,000 or $50,000 or more can rattle the nerves. The only way to do it is with utter confidence. I used to role-play asking for such large premiums in my head before asking the prospect in real life; I found this very therapeutic for the nervous system. I'll talk more about this type of exercise in an upcoming chapter, but for now, let me tell you a story from early in my career where my nerves almost got the better of me.

Well-endowed

It was the biggest break of my career and it came during my first year in the business. My manager asked me to deliver a $2,000 endowment check to one of our clients, Mr. Jones, the wealthy 65-year-old Welsh owner of a small pub and restaurant called The Tan Rabbit, as well as several other businesses.

As soon as I arrived I was taken upstairs to his small office, which was packed with cartons full of ketchup and had invoices and bills piled everywhere. Mr. Jones was standing in the middle of the only clear spot in the room when I walked through the door. He turned to me and growled, "Washrooms are downstairs. Follow the signs!"

"No, no!" I replied, already thrown for a loop by his harsh greeting. "I'm David Cowper, I'm from the New York Life Insurance Company and I...."

"Already got insurance," he snarled, "doesn't your office know that? What kind of morons am I dealing with here?"

"I'm here to deliver your endowment check, actually," I replied softly.

"Oh, well," he started, seeming to calm down a little, "that's okay. Here, clear yourself a seat and sit down."

I handed him his check, carefully moved a stack of papers, and sat down. He tore open the envelope, glanced at the check and then smiled. "Sorry, I was a little rude," he said. "I just thought you were lost or something. It's so hard to get anything done around here with all the interruptions." He gestured around the room, as if the mess proved his point.

As we talked I found out he had a wife, three kids and a brand-new grandson who had been born only two months earlier.

Seizing on that nugget of information, I said, "You know, Mr. Jones, you've benefited from this endowment plan, you should consider buying a similar plan to benefit your grandchild."

He paused before saying, "That's not a bad idea."

Although I was nervous about his temper returning at any second, I had been lucky so far, so I thought I would press on. "Maybe you should have endowment plans for your children as well," I suggested.

He thought that was quite a good idea too.

Being new to the business at that time, I didn't know how to go about putting such policies into action, so I left his office, promising to return with the paperwork. When I got back to my insurance company, I asked an agent who was good at the technical side of insurance to help me, and together we came up with five $70,000 policies, with a one-time premium of $200,000, which in those days was an astronomical amount. Today, it would be the equivalent of asking for a check for two or three million dollars and it made me very nervous. I felt he would surely lose his temper when we told him how much the policies would cost.

The next day, swallowing our terror, we drove over to The Tan Rabbit to close the deal. Mr. Jones led us up to his office, actually offered us coffee and then we started going over the policies. In the middle of explaining to him the benefits of the plans, we were interrupted by a waiter who wanted to change a light bulb downstairs. He sorted noisily though the assorted boxes strewn around the small office until he came to the carton containing the bulbs. I heard the clinking of glass while my colleague was speaking and looked up to see the waiter trying to lift an armload of bulbs at once. Suddenly his elbow caught on another cardboard box, his arms fell open and one of the bulbs crashed to the floor. The room erupted with a deafening pop.

Mr. Jones went crazy. He leaped from his chair and started screaming at the poor man. I thought he was going to assault him. We sat stone-faced and unbelieving while Mr. Jones ranted, accusing the waiter of all kinds of treachery. All of this for a mere 25-cent item. My colleague was beginning to pale, obviously thinking there was no way we'd be able to pick up a check for $200,000 from such a violent and stingy man.

The waiter hurried out under a rain of insults and vitriol. In my mind, I too cursed the waiter for bringing out the miser in Mr. Jones. As the door closed on the waiter's back, Mr. Jones returned his attention to us again. It was time to ask for the premium. I toyed with the idea of coming back at a later date, but realized that it was now or never. My stomach was roiling, and I was worried that when I spoke my voice would crack. I took a slow, deep breath and then, almost unconsciously, asked Mr. Jones, "We need a check for $200,000. You have to write it." I said it with such confidence that I surprised even myself.

He didn't say a word – he just wrote the check.

This moment proved to me that I had no reason to be nervous. If I have done my job – if I have prepared the case properly and sold the prospect on the benefits of the plan – the premium always follows.

An awesome presence

If you follow everything I showed you here in this chapter, you will be an awesome presence in a sales interview. When you sell the benefits, instead of the features, confront each objection head on, and reveal the logic of your solution, you are paving your way to the close. Then asking for the premium becomes a mere formality. This is certainly true for most business cases. But, if you are going to tackle megacases, there is still more to learn, much more. I could have followed everything I have discussed so far in this book and never sold a megacase were it not for another set of strategies – the strategies for persistence.

Four strategies for turning prospects into clients

1) SELL THE BENEFITS, NOT THE FEATURES.

2) CONFRONT EACH OBJECTION HEAD ON.

3) REVEAL THE LOGIC OF YOUR SOLUTION.

4) ASK FOR THE PREMIUM.

He was truly annoyed and

I scrambled for a way to salvage the

conversation. The only response

I could think of was to tell him,

"You don't understand my business."

"What do you mean?

I do understand your business,"

he replied, somewhat indignant.

"No," I said, "there is a saying in my business

– 'Nobody has endurance

like the person who sells insurance.'"

CHAPTER 9

Persistence in the megacase

P roper preparation and expert selling are keys to all insurance cases, but they are not everything. You need persistence. And nowhere is this more true than for megacases. In fact, in megacases, I consider preparation and selling to be the easy steps. It's persistence that's the challenge. Persistence is what you need to carry you through the long journey from the moment you set your sights on a megacase prospect, all the way to the final close – a journey that is many orders of magnitude more difficult than a small business-insurance case. In this chapter, I'll show you my strategies for persistence, and how I use them in my megacases, but first let me quickly sketch out some of the crucial benchmarks in the journey of a megacase.

The megacase journey

I usually first learn about a megacase prospect through my network or as a result of promoting myself. For example, in Chapter 3, I showed that my initial involvement in what became the $100,000,000 case was the result of a speech I gave at a financial conference. But once in the door, I must apply all my strategies for preparation and selling to their fullest. Wealthy prospects usually have very complicated business organizations and are often reluctant to discuss their business affairs. Disarming the prospect enough so that they divulge all the information I need is not a simple matter, and certainly demands persistence on my part. The prospect has to believe that it's necessary to discuss their business with me so that I'll be able to help. I then use all the information to zero in on the loss, expose it, and then present my solution. Then comes the barrage of objections from the prospect and all their advisors. I must successfully counter each objection and convince everyone that my solution makes financial and legal sense. Once they all agree to pursue my solution, I ask the prospect to sign an application – upgrading them from a mere prospect to an applicant. A signed application is certainly a benchmark, but is only the beginning of a long, often perilous, underwriting process.

Now that the prospect is an applicant, I have to convince them to go see a doctor – sometimes two doctors – for a full examination, blood tests, X-rays, and a stress test where, with electrodes hooked to their chests, they run to full capacity on a treadmill. If the medicals look good, I ask them to expose their private financial books to our inspectors and home office underwriters. I then have to get the client to cooperate with very inquisitive inspectors who want to make certain they don't indulge in any reckless or life-threatening behaviors, like heli-skiing, shark hunting, drug abuse, or sexual promiscuity. Needless to say, something can go wrong at any of the underwriting stages. The applicant might decide the whole process is too much of a hassle and give up. Life insurance is a wonderful financial tool, but it's not always easy to get; when someone wants massive amounts of it, they'd better be seriously committed. When the prospect or any of their advisors forgets how important the insurance is and begins expressing second thoughts, I often find myself reselling the entire case. But nurturing the applicant along the path to the ultimate close is only half the battle. In insurance megacases, I have to sell the case twice: once to the prospect, and a second time to the insurers.

The second sale

This second sale to the insurers is frequently the more difficult of the two sales. The insurer must be completely satisfied with all the applicant's results. But even with a fully insurable applicant, many insurers are cautious about taking on huge cases. And it's easy to see why. The risk is so much greater when a $20-million dollar payout is triggered by a single death, than when it is spread out over 20 or 30 separate deaths. That's why when an insurance company accepts one of my megacases, they have to go out and get their own insurance. This reinsurance process can easily jeopardize the deal. The immediate insurer acts only as a way station for the insurance. The reinsurers are a host of unseen judges who scrutinize every megacase. Even though the applicant and the immediate insurer agree to put the business on the books, oftentimes the reinsurer will balk.

If I am lucky, I measure the time it takes to meet a megacase prospect, upgrade him or her to an applicant, and then to a client in terms of months. More often, I measure it in years. Persistence is what it takes to hang in there that long. I have developed 5 strategies to help me persist: 1) Stick to your guns. 2) Warehouse your cases. 3) Keep calling. 4) Get outside the 9 dots. And 5) Walk away. In this chapter I'll show you how I used these strategies in actual cases, and how the 4th strategy helped me overcome some insurmountable obstacles in the $100,000,000 case.

Strategy 1: Stick to your guns

I take a long-term view of my business, which means I don't compromise my integrity for short-term gain. If I run into a prospect who wants me to sell them something I don't agree with, I will tell them to work with another agent. The prospect will now know one thing for sure – I am interested in doing what I feel is right, not simply in making a sale. When they see the degree of my conviction they may change their mind, or they may still go with another agent. If they do the insurance the way they want it with someone else, they will be doing the wrong insurance. If someday in the future, they realize their mistake, they may choose to come back to me. By sticking to my guns, I have won back cases that I lost years previously. Let me show you such a case.

Jack had the wrong insurance

I met Jack Bohlen, the major shareholder of a privately-held food company, when his chief financial officer, Vince, called me and a couple of other agents to look at the insurance coverage on Jack and the other shareholders. I stood a good chance of getting the business because I had known the chief financial officer for a few years. Before working for Jack, Vince was a partner at a small accounting firm, which was a client of mine. In fact, Vince still owned insurance that I had sold him.

All the agents were given a copy of the shareholder agreement and a synopsis of the current insurance coverage on the shareholders and asked to come back with a proposal. I went through it thoroughly but there certainly wasn't enough information to go on. I called Vince to learn more about the case.

"David," Vince said over the phone, "Jack's just looking for you to come back with quotes for the buy-out amounts listed in the agreement."

"But I need to know what Jack's plans are," I said. I had met Jack only once, very briefly, when I went to pick up the shareholder agreement and synopsis from Vince. Vince was going to courier the material to me, but I had insisted on coming in person because I wanted to meet Jack. Vince didn't seem thrilled with my idea, but agreed when I said that I simply wanted to shake his hand. When I arrived, Vince introduced me to Jack and we chatted for a few short moments. From that brief encounter, I was able to tell a few things from his personality. He was courteous, but aloof and not the type who tolerated fools. I was glad to have met him, but still needed to know much more about him.

"David," Vince said, "Jack's extremely cost-conscious. He really wants someone to restructure all the existing insurance, consolidate it—"

"He's looking to save money," I said.

"Exactly, David. You come in low, you'll get the deal."

"Vince," I said, "I'm not eager to get involved in a costing war, especially when I think I don't have all the facts."

"What is it you need to know?" Vince asked.

"Well, how long has he had the company? Did he start it himself?"

"Ten years, I think," Vince replied. "But he didn't start it; he bought it from somebody else."

"Was it big back then?"

"Yes."

"So there hasn't been much growth since he bought it, then?" I asked.

"Not really, David, but we are looking to see a lot of growth soon. Jack restructured everything, and pushed for a lot of the new items we're producing now. The new products just started hitting the market last year, and the initial growth is very positive."

"Where did he get the money to buy the company?"

"Jack's extremely wealthy. He made a ton in real estate and funneled some of his profits into buying this company."

"So, he's got a lot of other assets aside from this company?" I asked.

"Oh, yeah, quite a few properties, and a large stake in a mining company he helped raise capital for twenty years ago."

"What's it all worth?"

"Twenty-five million would be my guess."

"He's had a lot of growth on his capital, but not from the food company?"

"I guess so," Vince replied, then asked, "What are you getting at, David?"

"Is all the insurance he has listed in the synopsis?"

"Yes."

"And it's all term."

"Yes. You see, he's very money conscious – watches every dollar. That's why he's really hoping you can put something together that will save him."

"Don't worry, I'll save him money, but I can't do that with term insurance."

"What do you mean?"

"He's got a serious estate-tax problem. And it's not the shares in his company he should be worried about. It's everything else. When he dies, his estate will have to pay tax on 75% of all the gain on his properties and the mining stock."

"He can defer the tax until his wife dies."

"That's tax deferral, not tax elimination."

There was some silence on the other end of the phone.

"David," Vince said, "I think you should just come back with a simple quote based on the agreement. Jack's not interested in talking about insurance beyond that."

"Vince," I said, "I have to do my job."

Term insurance is like bed-wetting

The next day, I telephoned to speak with Jack.

"David," he said, when he picked up the phone, "I've put Vince in charge of the insurance, so you should just deal with him."

"But I'm not interested in the insurance, unless I can speak to you."

"I'm sorry to hear that," Jack replied stolidly.

"I'm sorry, as well. Vince seems to be interested in the most expensive insurance solution for you," I said.

I sensed Jack struggling with the idea of hanging up on me, but I knew I had piqued his curiosity with my last statement. "Pardon?" he said at last.

"He wants to go with term insurance, and only enough to cover your buy-sell agreement."

"And that's what I want too," Jack declared.

"And the government should be happy with that as well."

"Government?"

"The government is the heir to your estate, not your children."

"I don't want to talk about my estate, David. I have everything looked after."

"Jack, the least expensive way to pay off the government is through insurance. So your need for insurance is permanent, not temporary."

"I like term insurance, David. It's that simple."

Jack was stonewalling. I needed a way to penetrate his defense, a way to open his mind. "Jack," I said, "buying term insurance is like bed-wetting. Someday you have to wake up and change the sheets."

He laughed heartily at that, but his defenses remained staunchly intact. "I like that," he said, "but I must run. I'll look forward to seeing your proposal from Vince."

Holding out for a permanent solution

I never sent a proposal to Jack. Vince certainly wasn't going to champion my cause for permanent insurance, and I wasn't interested in trying to replace existing term insurance for cheaper term insurance. Jack had a serious need for insurance, and I wanted to solve his real problems. I wanted him to know that I wasn't going to compromise my position simply to get his business. I didn't think he would budge from his position, but I knew, at least, that he would gain some respect for me. I also knew that someday he would have to face up to his estate problem, and hoped that he would remember me.

Jack did pursue a restructuring of his term insurance with another agent. But because I kept Vince as a client for his personal insurance, I would visit him at his office occasionally and always made sure I popped in to see Jack. In my brief conversations with Jack I would always remind him that he had the wrong insurance. Once, he even asked me to repeat my bed-wetting remark so he could have a good laugh again. Although we were developing a rapport, there was still no sign of budging. I knew, however, that these occasional encounters would prevent him from forgetting about me, while I waited for the opportunity to make another serious bid for the business. That opportunity came a couple of years later when the company went through a restructuring phase. The insurance was again tendered out to a handful of agents, including me. Unfortunately, it was like re-living my earlier attempt. Jack simply wouldn't tolerate any discussion about permanent insurance, and everyone else, Vince, his advisors, and the other agents seemed to go along with him. Everyone but me, that is. Then, many years later, I received the call I had been waiting for.

"David," Vince said, "we need you to put $10,000,000 of insurance on Jack."

"Is Jack tendering the business again?" I asked

"No. He wants the insurance, and he wants it your way."

I knew that Jack was approaching his 65th year. Most of his term insurance was about to run out. Obviously, one of his advisors had woken up to the impending estate problem. Last I heard, Jack had $4 million in term coverage, but it would have been too late to convert it to permanent insurance. He should have done that before he turned 60. Getting new insurance at his age wouldn't be easy. I knew he was reasonably fit, but I thought it would be wise to apply for a lower amount, rather than go for too much at first and maybe not get any. "All right," I said to Vince, "but why don't we try for 3 or 4 million first. That way we can avoid some of the harsh medical tests. Given his age, I think the best approach would be to build up the insurance slowly."

"David," Vince said, "Jack wants 10." From the sound of his voice, I could tell that Jack wouldn't tolerate any alternatives. The stubbornness that was against me for so many years, was now turned fully in my favor.

I advised Jack to undergo all the medical tests necessary for the medical underwriting process to make certain he was insurable. It turned out that he was extremely healthy and would have no problem getting the full $10 million in coverage. Jack was pleased, and, of course, so was I. I had won Jack's confidence, but I hadn't yet won the case. The current agent, along with the other agents who had worked with Jack over the years, stepped in to vie for the business. I sensed that it wasn't going to be a cakewalk after all. I knew that I still had to come to the table with the best solution. The case turned out to be a real dogfight. I did eventually get the business, but only after applying some high-level strategies for closing megacases. I will be exploring what those strategies are in Chapter 11, and how I used them to close this case. But I can say one thing for sure – had I not stuck to my guns, I would never have had a shot. When I delivered the policies to Jack I said to him, "You certainly made me work for it, but I'm truly grateful."

"The reason I supported you, David," Jack replied, looking me straight in the eyes, "is because, over the years, you were the only agent who came in and told me I had the wrong insurance. You were right. Everyone else was trying to kiss my butt."

Strategy 2: Warehouse your cases

The agents who sold Jack Bohlen his term insurance failed to realize Jack's permanent need for insurance. If they had, they could have used the term insurance as a way to persist in the case. It's important to see term insurance as a tool for persistence when the prospect's need is permanent. If I'm involved in a case where the prospect is hesitant about committing to permanent insurance, I will push to put term in place in order to get the coverage and guarantee the client's insurability. But I make sure the client sees the term insurance as a stopgap measure. I call this warehousing my cases. Now that the insurance is in force, my challenge is to convert it at a later date. This can be difficult now that the client feels safely insured, but at least you are in control of the business. Jack's agents should have exposed his need for permanent insurance and urged him to convert his current coverage. Instead, they were afraid that by opposing Jack they might lose the case. Their lack of action left an opportunity that I seized upon, ultimately costing them the business. When you sell term insurance for a permanent need you are creating an opportunity for future business for yourself. Of course, you have to ensure that it's you who does the eventual conversion, not anyone else. The Dominic Gregory case I referred to in Chapter 8 was business that I had warehoused through term insurance.

I had originally approached Dominic after meeting him at a dinner party thrown by a mutual acquaintance. At the party we chatted about his investment company. He enjoyed discussing his business, and was particularly thrilled about discussing his dabblings with derivatives. Since I enjoyed listening to him, we hit it off pretty well. By the end of the evening, I had learned that he was quite wealthy and virtually without insurance. I suggested that we get together for lunch someday to see if there was any way I might be able to help him out. He agreed and we eventually did meet two months later at a downtown restaurant.

Insurance: a derivative
Over lunch, he told me that he had recently brought the topic of insurance up with his accountant who was an anti-insurance type. I told Dominic that I wouldn't try and sell him anything over lunch, and that put him at ease. I decided to raise the issue of insurance in a roundabout way.

"Dominic," I said, "you're fascinated with derivatives, aren't you?"

"Yes," he replied.

"How come?" I asked.

Dominic eagerly explained his love of derivatives. He seemed to revel in the idea that there was an invisible world of money that lay behind the real world of the marketplace and yet was so much larger than it. In the world of derivatives, people bet on the activities of the marketplace. With derivatives, you can make money even if market conditions worsen, so long as you bet that way. If you bet that the price of gold will drop $20 over the next four months, and it does just that, you win.

After a while, I said, "I'm in the derivatives business, too, Dominic." He looked a little puzzled. "Insurance is a derivative," I declared.

"How?"

"It's a derivative because its essence, as in all derivatives, is a bet. But instead of betting on behaviors related to the marketplace, insurance is a bet on a person's life – their time. When someone purchases life insurance from me it's like we're making a bet. On a million dollar policy, for example, I bet them $1,000,000 that they will not die this year. Let's say the annual premium is $10,000. In that case, they are betting me $10,000 that they will die before the year is up. And the bet can be renewed every year for the duration of the policy, so long as they pay the premium. Eventually they will die and they'll get the $1,000,000 layout, which makes it a smart bet. The risk of this single bet on one human life, is offset by spreading the risk over thousands of other lives. When someone buys life insurance they are really buying a derivative that is based on the complicated odds of when they and every other policyholder will die."

"I never thought of it like that," Dominic said.

"Insurance is a hedge against the risk of dying. And dying really means the loss of time. Time and risk are opposite sides of the same coin. After all, there would be no risk if their was no tomorrow. And conversely, the further out our time horizons, the greater the risk. What I do when I sell someone insurance is put a floor beneath them and their tomorrows. If there were no tomorrow, if the world were going to end at midnight tonight, how much insurance do you think I would sell? ... None."

Talking about insurance as a derivative seemed to enthrall Dominic. Our lunch discussion led to a meeting at his office two weeks later and an exploration of his estate and tax situation. I explained that insurance was the best way to pay the tax because it would pay a tax-free death benefit the moment the tax becomes payable. He liked the idea, but was not thrilled about paying whole life premiums, and neither was his accountant. I told Dominic that his need was permanent, that his estate problem wouldn't disappear when he turned 60 or 70.

Despite my efforts, he was reluctant to go ahead with my permanent insurance proposal. As a way of saving the case, and warehousing it for the future, I proposed term coverage. He agreed to the term coverage, but I knew that someday he would have to deal with the increasing premium and the eventual disappearance of coverage. As I described in Chapter 8, I eventually received a call from Dominic questioning the escalating premium. That call opened up the case again, and I was able, on that second go-around, to sell the permanent insurance.

Strategy 3: Keep calling

Getting an appointment with a megacase prospect is not an easy task, and demands persistence. Although it's always discouraging to get turned down for a meeting, I know that one phone call is rarely enough and that I'll have to keep trying before I succeed in getting an appointment. I am not the kind of person who aggressively browbeats a prospect. If the prospect does not want to meet me, I accept that, but I always try to leave the door open to approach them in the future. I will generally ask for permission to call them again when I have a new idea that might help them out. Most people will agree to that. As I said before, my perspective is long-term. I will chase a prospect for years, trying to build a relationship out of a string of phone calls. Because I know I only have a few moments over the phone, I tell them quickly why I am calling, and try to make my remarks as memorable as possible. When I call the prospect for a second time, months later, they will usually remember me. I am no longer a complete stranger. A few phone calls over the years can warm the prospect up enough to gain an appointment. It took me three years of continuous calling to get my third and crucial meeting with Rolf – the one I opened this book with – and Rolf was already more than a prospect, he was a client. Rolf tested the limits of my ability to persist. To give you an idea of what I went through to get that third meeting, I'd like to quickly tell you the story of my stormy relationship with Rolf.

Chasing Rolf

My first meeting with Rolf was during the $42 million case I discussed in Chapter 3. Although he was one of twelve partners in the company, he was obviously the most powerful of them all. No one had a majority share, but the other eleven partners clearly deferred to him as though he ran everything. I knew that any future business with this company would have to have his approval – he was the decision maker. So, after the $42 million was placed, I made a special effort to follow up with Rolf. I called him one afternoon and asked to see him with a proposal for personal coverage. He agreed to see me.

The second meeting with Rolf: instant premium

I arrived at his office a few minutes ahead of time for our 8:00 AM meeting and waited in the lobby. At 8:00 sharp I was ushered into a boardroom where Rolf sat at the end of a massive oak table.

"Good morning, Rolf," I said.

"Morning," he replied in a way that indicated he didn't want to pursue a personal conversation. This was my second physical meeting with Rolf. He wasn't personable in the first meeting, and he hadn't warmed up much in the meantime. He was a business machine, and unwilling to tolerate a wasted moment, or any weakness in the people he dealt with. So, immediately following our brief salutations, I laid out on the table in front of him a proposal for a million dollars of personal insurance, and with an almost mechanical manner I quickly told him how it worked, why he needed it, and how this insurance would act as a foundation, upon which we could build in the future. He looked at the proposal for a few seconds, and then said, "Yes."

I pulled out an application, and asked him whether there had been any changes to his health since the recent underwriting.

"No," he replied instantly.

I opened the application and pointed to the signature line. "Sign here."

Rolf uncapped his fountain pen, signed, and then stood up to leave.

"I'll need a check for the premium, Rolf," I said with conviction.

He stopped in his tracks, reached over to the phone that lay in the middle of the boardroom table and pressed the intercom button.

"Mr. Cowper needs a check," he said, then turned to me, "That was Helen, she will do as you wish."

Rolf left the room, and I sat there mesmerized. It seemed too easy. After a moment, I placed the application in my briefcase and went looking for Helen. Ten minutes later I left Rolf's building with a signed application and a check for the premium. It was so easy.

In the car on the drive back to my office, I reflected on the meeting. I had never met anybody like Rolf before. He was the kind of client you both feared and loved. If he liked what you showed him, he would make his decision with lightning speed, but if he found a mistake in your work, he would cut you out of his life. He was for you, or against you. With no in-between. Today he was for me, but I was soon to find out what being on the other side was like.

A few months after placing the extra million on Rolf, I wanted to follow up again with another meeting. I was hoping to do a detailed examination of his estate and then make a recommendation for a more complete portfolio of insurance. I made a few phone calls, but none were returned. I kept trying for a few weeks, and still no response. I didn't know what to think. I knew Rolf was exceptionally busy, but I did expect him to return my call. At last, I figured that I was probably too far down his list of priorities, so I decided to lay off for a few months.

Cancellation

When I called back in a few months, my luck was no better. But then early the next year Rolf called me.

"I want to cancel the million dollar policy," he said to me over the phone.

"May I ask why?" I said.

"Because I want to cancel it."

I stifled my panic, and said, "You have some cash value in the policy, so I'll need you to sign a cancellation form so you can get your money."

"I don't want to sign anything," he stated firmly.

"But your money–"

"I don't want the money," he said and hung up.

A feeling of dread filled me. My biggest policyholder just canceled his personal business with me, and wouldn't tell me why. I began to panic about the company insurance. Was Rolf going to cancel all that as well? I prayed hard. After a few minutes of mental anguish I managed to calm my thoughts, and tried to figure out why he canceled the insurance and why he was so curt with me. As hard as I tried I really couldn't summon up a satisfactory answer – I simply didn't know. The best guess I had was that he was somehow upset with me, but I didn't know why. I decided to place a call to the accountant to see if anything had come up regarding the insurance on the partners. I got a hold of the accountant, Edward Lerouz, later in the day and talked briefly with him. I didn't mention the phone call from Rolf, but asked if there were any recent movements that might affect the insurance. He said no. I was slightly relieved, but still concerned. I still had to figure out what to do with Rolf's policy. In the end, I effected a paid-up policy with the cash value. Rolf no longer had to pay premiums, and, as was his wish, he never received the surrender value.

Weeks passed and nothing came up about the business insurance, so I began to sleep better. I did, however, occasionally call Mr. Lerouz to chat briefly about the company. A year later, in one of our telephone conversations, Mr. Lerouz informed me that a major restructuring of the partnership was being planned.

According to Lerouz, 7 of the 12 partners wanted to sell their share in the company to 5 new people. When the sale was complete, there would be 10 partners instead of 12, and Rolf would remain as the strongest partner. I asked Lerouz if they were going to fund the buyout with loans, and he said yes. Then I asked him what the size of the loans were expected to be. He replied $30 million. The 7 partners who were selling had smaller interests in the partnership than the remaining 5. I did some quick math in my head to try and figure out the growth of the company since I originally did the insurance. Then I calculated what the current insurance need would be. The answer I came up with was $100,000,000. I almost slid off my chair onto the floor.

"Edward," I said, "when are they going ahead with the buyout?"

"I'm not sure, but I know they are planning it now."

"We'll have to underpin those loans with insurance. And we'll have to get new insurance on the original partners to reflect the new value of the company."

"David," Edward said, "you'll have to speak to Rolf."

Edward was right – any new insurance needed Rolf's patronage. I was not looking forward to calling Rolf again, but I knew I had to. He and the rest of the partners were clearly underinsured. Collectively their net worth had more than doubled in the past few years. To get the new business, I would have to reestablish my relationship with Rolf.

I placed a call to Rolf later in the afternoon. A week went by without a return call, and I tried again. This time I happened to get him live on the phone. It was an oversight on the part of the receptionist. I think she assumed I was somebody else and put me through.

"Yes," Rolf said.

"Hello, Rolf, it's David Cowper–"

"Yes," Rolf said, his tone harsher this time.

"I have an insurance concept I'd like to show you – a zero-cost insurance plan." It was a new concept that I had recently developed where the death benefit consisted of the original face amount plus the premiums plus the interest those premiums would have earned. I had successfully sold zero-cost insurance to other clients; I wanted to show it to Rolf and win back his confidence. If I could do this type of plan with him on a personal basis, I would stand myself in good stead for the new partnership insurance.

"I don't have time," he replied.

"I understand. How about I call you in a couple of months to see if you'll be able to find time then."

There was a short pause. "Fine," he replied.

The person who has endurance

I called a couple of months later and managed to get him on the phone again, but had a similar experience. In fact, I kept up the routine for another year and half, until finally the script changed. Instead of telling me he was busy, he said, "You're a pest."

He was truly annoyed and I scrambled for a way to salvage the conversation. The only response I could think of was to tell him, "You don't understand my business."

"What do you mean? I do understand your business," he replied, somewhat indignant.

"No," I said, "there is a saying in my business – 'Nobody has endurance like the person who sells insurance.'"

There was silence for a second and my heart raced, and then I heard him laugh. "You're really serious," he said.

"Yes," I replied, my pulse subsiding.

"What time do you get up in the morning?"

"You name whatever time you like, and I'll be up before you."

"Seven o'clock. I'll be going to the airport, but I'll meet you on the highway and you can have fifteen minutes."

Zero-cost insurance

As I showed you in chapter 1, we arranged to rendezvous on the shoulder of a particular stretch of highway close to the airport. During this meeting, Rolf showed no sign that he had ever harbored any ill feelings towards me. It was all behind us now, and I knew I would never discover his reasons for canceling the insurance or ignoring my phone calls. In the limo, I showed Rolf a set of six different proposals, variations on a zero-cost insurance plan. Normally, I would never present this many, but I knew Rolf would want it that way. He would want to see all his options and assess them himself. It literally took him only seconds to study all the proposals and make his selection. And, of course, it was the right choice.

He chose a plan with an original face amount of $2 million dollars. Rolf would pay premiums for 10 years and have a paid-up policy. The face amount would grow by the amount of the premiums paid in, plus an amount that represented what those premiums would have earned at a 4% annual compound rate. His ultimate real cost of the insurance would be the difference between the 4% and what he would otherwise earn on those premiums had he invested them elsewhere. Given that Rolf was in the 50% tax bracket, the 4% was more like earning 8%, because if he invested his money outside the insurance plan, he would have to pay tax on the growth. So, it really was as close as you could get to a zero-cost insurance plan. Rolf liked the concept.

I was counting on Rolf making his mind up quickly, because what I really wanted to do was introduce the topic of the partnership insurance. I still had a few minutes left, and I knew Rolf would give them to me. He had agreed to fifteen minutes, I would have my time, but no more. We discussed the financing of the new partnership arrangement and how the need for insurance had grown to $100,000,000. I told Rolf that we could do the insurance on the same zero-cost basis. He agreed to arrange a meeting with his accountants and lawyers to discuss it further.

Over the next few weeks I had several meetings with Rolf and his advisors. The need for the insurance was glaringly obvious, so no one was questioning it. The type of insurance was another matter. There were many questions from the accountants and the lawyers, and concern over the large premium. I was eager to underwrite the case and put some insurance in force, so I adopted my strategy for warehousing and suggested we move ahead on 5-year-renewable-and-convertible term insurance. Everyone agreed to this. But, as in most megacases, this agreement was still miles away from a close. In megacases, the most trying challenges often come when selling the case to the insurance company – the underwriting process. Here is where I ran into crippling problems. It took another strategy of mine to overcome obstacles that would have certainly killed the deal. That strategy is my fourth and most important strategy for persistence. However, before I get to it, I have a little puzzle for you.

The 9 dots

You may already be familiar with this puzzle, but if you are not, you should try it out. The challenge is to link up all the 9 dots using only 4 straight lines without lifting your pencil off the paper.

If you managed to solve the puzzle, congratulations. You are ready for megacase selling! If you were stumped, turn to the end of this chapter for the answer. You will see that the solution requires you to 'get outside the 9 dots.' This phrase may ring a bell with you because it is used to refer to creative thinking, or as Edward de Bono, a modern-day Socrates, calls it – Lateral Thinking. I owe the closing of many megacases to creative problem solving, so that's why my next strategy is called 'Get outside the 9 dots.'

Strategy 4: Get outside the 9 dots

With the 9-dots problem, nearly everyone begins to solve the problem by starting with one of the dots, and staying within the 9 dots as they draw their line. But staying within the 9 dots is not a constraint of the puzzle. It is a self-imposed constraint. You can arrive at the solution only when you realize that the space outside the 9 dots is part of the puzzle and available for your exploration. In other words, a solution is possible only when you realize that the constraint you were working under is not really a constraint at all. It is the same in many megacase problems, where finding a solution means discovering which constraints are real and which are imaginary.

When a prospect or client raises a deal-breaking objection that cannot be solved under the traditional constraints in our business, I know I must get outside the 9 dots. If I try to sell the case by skirting their objection, I will lose the deal. Although confronting these types of objections is nerve-wracking, I see them as an opportunity to add value and justify why the client needs me. Let me show you some of the objections and how I dealt with them in the $100,000,000 case.

Mission impossible

When Rolf and his team of advisors agreed to the proposal for term insurance, I experienced a fleeting moment of relief. I had been chasing Rolf for years for the opportunity to broker the new partnership insurance. But there was a long way to go, and I knew I didn't have the luxury of relaxing. The day after I received the go ahead I called Edward Lerouz, the accountant.

"Edward," I said, "we'll need the company's audited statements for the financial underwriting."

"Sorry, David, I can't do that." I closed my eyes. I had dreaded this answer. I knew that Rolf and his partners were extremely private about their business, but I had hoped they would understand the need to cooperate with the insurance company's underwriting requirements.

"Edward, no insurance company will issue the amounts we want without audited statements. You can't ask an insurance company to accept $100,000,000 of risk, without doing their due diligence. They have to be absolutely certain the company is worth that amount."

"David, I understand the problem, but there is simply no way Rolf will agree to releasing audited statements.... Listen, why don't you ask him yourself."

"Thanks, Edward." I hung up the phone and sat back in my office chair. Without proper financial underwriting, there would be no insurance, no $100,000,000 case. Half of me wanted to call Rolf right away to confirm the problem, the other half wanted to hang onto the glimmer of hope that Rolf would cooperate. A few moments later I was still leaning back in my chair, pondering, when my wife Teri came into the office. She had come by to meet me for lunch.

Smiling, she walked over and gave me a kiss, then took a seat across from my desk. I was obviously lost in a mental stupor.

"David, are you okay?"

"Fine," I answered unconvincingly.

Teri looked at me knowingly. "What is it?" she asked.

"The case–"

"What about it?" she asked with concern. Teri followed my business very closely and was familiar with my pursuit of Rolf. She had been ecstatic when I received the go-ahead. She knew it wouldn't be easy, but was optimistic.

"They don't want to give us their financial statements," I said.

"Oh," she replied, happiness draining from her face.

We were both quiet for a while, then Teri asked, "Can you do the insurance without them."

"No.... I don't see how."

Teri summoned up a smile, "You'll figure something out, David. You always do."

"I know," I said, trying to conceal the doubt that was eating my insides. I didn't want her to worry, so I returned her smile, and suggested we head out for our lunch.

After lunch, I returned to the office and placed my call to Rolf.

"Rolf," I said, "I understand your concern for privacy. The insurance companies are extremely careful with sensitive data. Your statements will be safe."

"David," Rolf said, "we can make other information available to you, but we do not issue audited statements."

"Without them it's difficult to find insurance."

"Then we won't do the deal," he said flatly.

"I didn't say it was impossible, I said it would be difficult." I, of course, had no idea whether it was possible or not, but I didn't want Rolf to think the deal was off.

I respected Rolf's concern for privacy, so I knew it was a real objection, not an excuse to avoid doing the insurance. The solution to the problem would not lie in trying to find a way to convince Rolf to furnish the insurer with audited statements. That would be like trying to connect the 9 dots by staying within the square. I had never heard of a case of this size being approved without audited statements. But it would have to be done. I had to approach the problem by exploring the area 'outside the square.'

I put myself in the shoes of the insurer and asked why they required audited statements. The answer was they needed assurance that the financial information stated in the applications was true. But maybe there was another way to satisfy the insurer. After I hung up the phone with Rolf, I started telephoning the head underwriters of all the insurers I dealt with and asked them whether they would consider alternatives to audited statements.

The first five I called said there would be absolutely no way they would do the insurance without the audited statements. But Steven, the head underwriter at the sixth company I called, said they would be open to alternatives. That's what I was looking for – an opening, no matter how small. Now all I had to do was come up with the alternative. To do that, I would need to relax and think creatively.

I told my secretary to hold my calls for the next twenty minutes, and went to lie down on the couch at the far end of my office. I tucked a pillow under my head, put my feet up on the armrest, and shut my eyes. I could see an orange glow as the fluorescent light from the ceiling filtered through my eyelids. I thought of being on a beach in Florida and listening to the waves lapping onto the sand. I began to relax. I wanted to remove all my anxieties about the case, so I could think clearly and objectively. But, in order to discover a satisfactory alternative to the audited statements, I would also have to think the way a home-office underwriter thinks.

When I felt ready, I mentally transformed myself into an underwriter, and asked myself what it would take to remove my doubts about the company's financials. I meditated on the question for a few minutes. Not getting audited statements meant not getting anything in writing. But maybe an underwriter wouldn't need anything in writing. Thousands of business deals are done on a handshake. And a handshake works so long as you trust the person. Perhaps I could win the underwriter's trust by finding a third party to vouch for Rolf. Surely Rolf's bankers had done their own due diligence and satisfied themselves that he would be able to pay off the $100,000,000 loan. The underwriter would approve the insurance if assured by Rolf's bankers that the company financials were correct. I was thrilled. That's how we would underwrite the case.

I rose from the couch and called Steven, the underwriter. I suggested a meeting between him and his corporate secretary and Rolf's accounting firm and bankers. He liked the idea, so I phoned Rolf to get his approval. He was supportive and willing to cooperate.

Three weeks later, the meeting took place, which, in deference to Rolf's concern over privacy, I did not attend. Instead, I waited nervously by the phone in my office for the verdict. Four hours after the meeting began, I received the call. The insurer was satisfied. However, we still weren't home, the approval from the reinsurers was still required. But, thanks to Steven, that eventually was achieved. By this time, the medical underwriting was completed and approved. So the deal was closed, or so it seemed, until another objection was raised.

Premium nightmare

After I heard the news about the final reinsurance approval,
I telephoned Rolf to arrange for the premium.

"David, we'd like to pay monthly," he said. I knew that the only
way an insurance company would accept monthly billing would be
on an automatic withdrawal basis. Even though a client would pay
around 10% more for the privilege of paying monthly, the insurer
claimed that processing monthly checks still cost them too much.

"We'll have to arrange for the insurer to automatically withdraw
the premium from your bank account," I said.

"No you won't."

"But—"

"No one gets access to our bank account," Rolf stated.

"Would you consider paying any other way – annually, semi-
annually, quarterly?" I asked.

"No. Why would I give the insurance company all that money
up front?" I understood Rolf's point. By paying monthly he would
have the rest of the year's premium to make investments with. Given
the size of the premium, the opportunity costs were significant.

"I understand," I said.

When I finished with Rolf, I telephoned Steven and asked him if
he could make a special arrangement to accept the premium in
monthly checks. He said he didn't think it was possible, but would
do everything he could to make it happen. After a few days, Steven
phoned with the bad news – they were sorry but they simply would
not take monthly checks. From their point of view, they had enough
flexibility in their premium payment methods, and they insisted that
if Rolf wanted the insurance, he should have no trouble paying
according to one of their accepted methods.

I couldn't believe that I had come this close to the finish line only
to confront another deal breaker. Rolf and the insurance company
would not budge from their positions. It was a total impasse. There
was no traditional solution available. I would have to get outside the
9 dots again. I returned to my couch to meditate, and arose a half
hour later with the answer. I telephoned Steven with my proposal.

"Steven," I said, "if Rolf won't give you access to his account,
maybe we should do it the other way around."

"What do you mean?" Steven asked, perplexed.

"Give Rolf access to your account."

There was silence.

"Well," Steven began, "we've never done this before, of course, but I don't see why not."

Now all I had to do was get Rolf's approval. I telephoned Rolf and told him the idea. "You can put the insurance company on your payroll, and deposit the premium into their account."

"Yes, David, we'll do it like that."

And that's how the $100,000,000 megacase was finally closed.

Strategy 5: Walk away

Before I close this chapter, I would like to discuss my last strategy for persistence. In fact, it is the flip-side of persistence – walking away.

The lure of the megacase market is mighty. Whenever I hear about a prospect who is in the market for $30,000,000, or $50,000,000 of insurance, my heart flutters. But I know better than to just dive right in. I must do my due diligence and follow the strategies for preparing the case as though it were a case for $100,000. If I get too excited and leap into the middle of the case, I risk wasting my time. I may find out in the end that there really was no case in the first place, and had I done my preparation I would have realized that. The megacase market reminds me of the ancient Greek stories of the Sirens – mermaids who, with their beautiful voices, tempted sailors to leap from their ships onto the treacherous rocks. An agent must always watch themselves, to ensure that they do not fall prey to their own vain wishes and end up on the rocks.

But even when you try your best to do your due diligence, you can still be led astray. Megacases are extremely complex and it is often difficult to prepare the case as well as you might wish. The strategy that causes me the most heartache is finding the decision maker. Whenever I have walked away from a megacase it was because of my failure to find the decision maker. Unfortunately, I was often in quite deep before I realized the problem. Ultimately, however, no matter how much you have sweated over the case, if you cannot find the decision maker, you must walk away.

The red herring

I once spent many months chasing a $300,000,000 annuity. I was invited into the case by another agent, who hoped that I would be able to work some magic and close the deal. It was a globe-trotting case, and I eventually ended up playing hop-scotch on the map of Europe – flying from France to Luxembourg. Luxembourg to

Germany. After a half-dozen flights and many long distance calls, I could not, despite my best efforts, find the decision maker.

We had been dealing with an ambassador for the prospect, and I had asked him many times for the opportunity to speak to the prospect directly. He always promised me a meeting, but was forever breaking his promises. Eventually, I realized that I would never speak to the decision maker, and decided to walk away. The other agent was devastated at the thought of throwing away a $300,000,000 case, as was I, but I knew there was no deal, and I didn't want to waste another minute of my valuable time.

The tickle-me-David prospect

Sometimes the problem isn't that you can't find the decision maker, it's that you found the decision maker and they're incapable of making a decision. This has happened to me a number of times.

Once I worked on a case for a $20,000,000 policy. The prospect was very generous throughout the entire process. He showed nothing but enthusiasm for the case, and the sale seemed like it would be a cinch. But I began to get a little suspicious when the prospect kept postponing our final meeting. He was courteous about the postponements: "David," he would say, "I'm sorry, I've just gotten so busy this week. Let's do it next week, I promise." Next week he would cancel, and so on for six weeks straight. By then I had put so much into the deal, and was looking forward to the final close. In fact, at the time, I really needed the money. But after seven weeks, I stopped calling. If he was serious, he could call me.

We never spoke again.

Hunting elephants

I hunt elephants. Megacases, like elephants, are rare. When you do find one, you have to make it count. I depend on closing megacases, because I may go months without a sale, and during these droughts my cash flow may dry up. That's why I pour everything I have into them. The experience is often an emotional roller-coaster. But I have faith in the strategies that I have developed, and I know that if I follow them, if I stick to my guns, warehouse my cases, keep calling, and get outside the 9 dots, I stand the best chance of getting the close. But I persist in a case only when I have faith that the ultimate close is attainable. If I don't have that faith, I walk away. And to me, knowing when to walk away is just as crucial as knowing when to hang in.

Five strategies for persisting in the megacase

1) STICK TO YOUR GUNS.

2) WAREHOUSE YOUR CASES.

3) KEEP CALLING.

4) GET OUTSIDE THE 9 DOTS.

5) WALK AWAY.

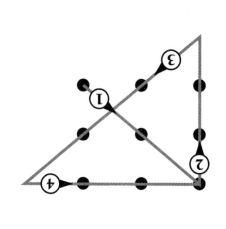

HERE IS THE SOLUTION TO THE 9-DOTS PROBLEM.

PART IV

How to become a mega-agent

In an almost desperate voice,

I turned to Huss and asked him,

"You've seen agents come and go over the years,

what does it take to be successful

in this business?"

He paused, looked briefly

at the ceiling and said,

"Plan your work and work your plan."

That was it.

CHAPTER 10

Visualization

Before I ever sold a policy, before I ever became the top salesperson in my branch, before I ever qualified for the Million Dollar Round Table, or the Top of the Table, or sold a $100,000,000 of insurance, I saw them in my mind first.

Our minds are where we forge our entire lives. Our friends, the people we marry, the careers we choose – they are all predicated on how we see ourselves in our minds. We live the lives we subconsciously believe we deserve. You cannot live big if there is a voice in your head that says you are small. For a lucky few, thinking big is natural; for the rest of us, we have to work at it. And I work at it every day of my life.

In chapter 2, I showed you how I managed to survive in the early part of my career by seeing myself today as I wanted to be tomorrow and by developing plans to make my future a reality. These strategies were just the beginning. In this chapter, I will show you the 5 strategies I developed later to help me, not just survive, but excel as a mega-agent: 1) Visualize your goals. 2) Plan your work and work your plan. 3) Train your brain for success. 4) Visualize the case. 5) Use visualization to solve a megacase crisis.

Strategy 1: Visualize your goals

It is impossible for an agent to think small and sell big, and it's just as impossible for an agent to think big and sell small. With this statement in my mind, I have forced myself to think big. And the first strategy in thinking big is seeing it in your mind. You have to make the abstract notion of success something concrete by visualizing a specific goal. Let me show you an example from my early years where this kind of visualization helped make my big thoughts a reality.

The production board

When I was first starting out in the insurance business as an agent for the New York Life Insurance Company, there was a massive production board in the open office we all shared. This board ruled our lives, names moved up and down according to our weekly sales, fortunes rose and fell. The men and women with the skill and perseverance to stay at the top of the board were the office celebrities, making money, joking with management, buying fashionable clothes and driving top-of-the-line cars. As a rookie agent, with very few sales under my belt, I was stuck on the bottom rung of the ladder. In the early weeks of my career I stuttered and faltered through difficult cold calls and just as cold sales meetings. Everyone else in the office seemed to be screaming through their networks, bringing in handfuls of policies every week.

I worked hard from Monday to Friday, but I did my most important work on Saturday. On Saturday morning, I would sit in front of the production board and stare. I was alone in the office, sitting upright in my swivel chair, head supported on my hands, my eyes riveted to that board. I saw every name, knew every dollar amount from every sale that each agent had made. But I saw one thing differently – I saw my own name at the top of the list. That was my goal: to be the number-one producer for our branch. I pictured the production board with 'David Cowper' printed in the yellow, block numeral one.

To become number one, I knew I would have to do more than just visualize.

Strategy 2: Plan your work and work your plan

The commandment

Once, during my tenure at the bottom of the production ladder, I had the privilege of a brief meeting with Huss, my first manager.

We were seated across from each other in his office. I could see beyond him through the window that looked out over the cubicles the agents inhabited. Several of them hunkered down over their phones. They reminded me of lab animals participating in a behavioral experiment. Like well-trained creatures, they would pick up the phone, speak, put it down and dial again – over and over again. Suddenly I felt very heavy. I was one of them, and the one most likely to be weeded out of the experiment. In an almost desperate voice, I turned to Huss and asked him, "You've seen agents come and go over the years, what does it take to be successful in this business?"

He paused, looked briefly at the ceiling and said, "Plan your work and work your plan." That was it.

That simple point is the real key to visualization – it's no good to sit around dreaming all day. You need to develop a plan for reaching your goals and then you have to execute it.

My plan for getting to the top of the ladder

On the weekend after my meeting with Huss, I locked myself in my apartment and set myself the task of specifically developing a plan that would get me to the top of the ladder. I needed a plan that was easy to follow, and one with clear benchmarks, so I could gauge my performance. After a few hours of brainstorming, I came up with a package approach to insurance.

The essential ingredient of my plan was something I called 'a unit.' The unit was a quote for $100,000 of insurance. And I had a set of units for people aged 30, 35, 40, and 45. My plan was this – each month I would sell one entire unit, two half units, four quarter units, and 10 tenths of a unit.

My approach was as follows: whenever I met a prospect, I would always produce the $100,000 unit and say, "I'm showing you a unit. Take a look at it and see if you like it. If you do, you can have half a unit, a quarter, or 10 percent of it – that is a decision only you can make." And to reach a little higher than my stated plan, I would sometimes say to a prospect that they could even double the unit.

This approach gave me the opportunity to ask a lot of prospects to buy a full unit. For the first couple of months, I never achieved my plan. I sold a number of one-tenth units and the odd quarter unit. But after a couple of months, I sold more quarters and the occasional half unit, then a lot of quarters and a few halves. Finally, in the fifth month I sold my first full unit. And shortly after that a double unit. And by that time, I had moved to the top of the production ladder.

The importance of milestones in a plan

If your vision is too big and not measurable it will be almost impossible to achieve. That's why you need an effective plan. The key to any successful plan is that it should be made up of a number of benchmarks you can measure yourself against on a regular basis. It's easier to accomplish a hundred small things that add up to your vision, than to try to realize your vision on one giant case right out of the gate. The trick is that each step must make a contribution to the overall plan.

The old story is: a traveler in Ancient Greece saw a man sitting on the roadside. "Pardon me?" the traveler asked, "How do I get to Mount Olympus?" The man he asked happened to be Socrates who replied sagely, "Just make sure that every step you take goes in that direction."

Strategy 3: Train your brain for success

After I reached the top of the production board I set other goals for myself. For a while, one goal was like the holy grail for me – the million-dollar policy. As I grew in the business, that goal seemed more and more realistic, and one afternoon in the mid-'60s I decided to set my mind to it.

My first million-dollar case

I was seated at a desk, an expensive and heavy pen in my right hand, an insurance application in front of me. In the bottom corner of the page, the line listing the face value of the policy said, '$1,000,000.' Wow. My heart skipped a beat.

Carefully, breathing deeply and trying to keep my hand steady, I penned in the client's name in the space provided, 'Samuel V. Karsh.' Beside his name I filled in his birth date, 'August 19, 1909,' then skipped a line and, with a smile, wrote, 'company president' beside occupation. I sat and just stared at the pages in front of me for a moment. I couldn't take my eyes off the figure, '$1,000,000.' My heart raced and my stomach felt light.

Suddenly, a voice came over my left shoulder, "Hi David, I.... oh, you're filling in an application! How much is it for?"

I was so absorbed by the application in front of me that I hadn't heard someone approaching me from behind. It was Bernard Stoles, a friend and fellow agent.

"It's for a million dollars," I said.

"Wow! You sold a million-dollar case?" he replied, clapping me on the shoulder and then giving a low whistle. "I didn't know you were working on a case that big. That's incredible!"

I put down my pen, let out a deep breath and turned to face him. The tension drained from my shoulders and a smile crossed my face.

"Sorry, Bernie, dinner isn't on me tonight," I responded." I haven't sold a million, I'm just filling in the application."

"Just filling in the app?" he asked, shooting me a puzzled look.

"Well, it's good practice," I said. "When I do write a million-dollar policy I don't want my hand to shake." At this point I opened the bottom drawer of my desk and tossed the application on top of a pile of other applications.

"What are all those?" Bernie inquired, referring to the stack of applications.

"Other million-dollar apps," I said.

He looked at me incredulously, "What? Why are you doing this?" he exclaimed.

"Just for practice," I explained. "When I do sell my first real million-dollar case, I'll throw them all out."

The real million-dollar story

Later that year I did write my first million-dollar application, but for financial reasons it was declined. However, I wasn't disappointed because I had finally written one in front of an actual prospect and convinced him to sign it. For all intents and purposes I had closed a million-dollar case. I just hadn't been paid.

It wasn't until three years later that I wrote my first million-dollar case and followed it through to completion. That turned out to be the case that involved six different developers that I described in detail in chapter 6. In fact, it wasn't just my first $1 million-dollar case; I ended up placing a million-dollar policy on each of the six, for a total of $6,000,000.

The practical reason for practicing big ideas

Many people would consider filling out all those imaginary million-dollar applications a waste of time. Shouldn't I have been out there prospecting? But my primary motivation for filling out all those apps was a very practical one – I didn't want to be nervous when I actually found myself across the table from a million-dollar prospect and had to fill in the policy amounts. I was confident I would eventually write one but I was concerned my hands would shake so badly that I wouldn't even be able to write legibly.

I also believe there was a more mystical benefit to filling in those imaginary applications. In my view, there is a part of the mind that can't distinguish well between the imaginary and the real. When I filled in those applications, I fooled that part of my mind into believing million-dollar policies were a regular occurrence. And because the mind is where we forge our lives, million-dollar policies did become a reality for me.

I have shown you how I use visualization to reach the large goals in my life, but I also use it on a case-by-case basis. Let me show you how, through visualization, I closed a case involving issues similar to the Lindrum, Weirnicke, and Bantam case we saw in Chapter 6.

Strategy 4: Visualize the case

The $12 million Clifton case

Mr. Clifton leaned across his desk. I could see his nostrils flaring and eyes growing wide. "Mr. Cowper," he said, "do you really expect me to believe that I need 12 million dollars of insurance? I have properties that are worth far more than that right now. Surely when I die, we can use those assets to pay off the estate taxes."

I didn't flinch. His question was a good one. I had been chasing this man for months, trying time and time again to set up this meeting. I knew he needed the insurance I was proposing. If I wanted to walk out of his office with the premium I would have to overcome his objections by revealing the logic of my solution.

"Mr. Clifton, there are three ways to settle your account with the government when you die," I said. "Unfortunately you are not very liquid – your assets are all tied up in the buildings and land you own. So, at death, you can pay your taxes by: 1) selling one of your properties, 2) borrowing against your assets, or 3) from the proceeds of a life insurance policy.

"As you suggest, you could sell one of your properties, but then you deprive your heirs of the future growth of that asset. Once sold, it becomes someone else's asset and any increase in value that is gained after your death is lost to your wife and children. Remember that there is always a market for your best assets, but you'll then be left with the worst assets, the very assets that are draining your cash. It's very likely that the property you'll be forced to sell is not the one you want to lose."

"Hmmmm," he replied, "Well, what about borrowing then?" Before I entered the picture Mr. Clifton had never really considered the dispersal of his assets after his death. He was a fairly young man, and with any luck that day was still some time away. But, I could see he was beginning to understand the issues that lay ahead for him. He folded his arms and leaned back in his chair to listen.

"If you borrow against your assets," I started, "you would have to pay back that loan with after-tax dollars...."

Suddenly, my train of thought was shattered by the loud blare of a car horn. I turned quickly and looked over my right shoulder. Through the back window of my car I could see a small Toyota Corolla stopped behind my right rear bumper. The driver was gesturing at me madly. When I turned back, Mr. Clifton had vanished. In fact, he had never really been there at all – at least not in reality.

The car horn had interrupted the visualization exercise I go through prior to every sales meeting I have. I glanced quickly at my watch and realized it was actually time for my meeting with Mr. Clifton. I waved back to the driver in the Corolla, indicating that I was parking my car, switched off the ignition and hurried inside to sell another megacase.

Practical reasons for visualizing the case

You saw in chapter 7 how thoroughly I like to prepare for every sales meeting. One of the key strategies I have for ensuring that every meeting goes well is repeatedly visualizing how the meeting will unfold before I ever enter the prospect's office. As you saw in the Mr. Clifton example, I imagine the prospect, the details of their office, and then I completely immerse myself in the dialogue we are likely to have.

In the visualization process, I anticipate every objection the prospect might have with my plan. Then, when I'm sure I've come up with more objections than the prospect will actually raise, I construct answers or solutions to each one and begin to role-play the objections and answers in my mind. I am rarely ruffled by a client, no matter how egregious their behavior, because I have seen every outcome of that meeting in my imagination already.

I run through the entire meeting, from the second I say hello and shake the prospect's hand to the moment I leave with the premium check in my briefcase. For days before a sales meeting I will spend every spare second running through the meeting again and again, honing my answers, testing for unforeseen objections. In fact, I always plan my time before a meeting so that I can arrive early, sit in my car and have one final run-through. When I hit the prospect's office I am as confident as any trial lawyer on court day or thespian walking on stage to the first lines of *Hamlet*.

The practical benefit to this type of context-specific visualization is that it helps immunize me against a prospect's objections and, as a result, I'm not surprised by their questions. I give smooth, well-rehearsed answers, which add to the impression that I am well-prepared, competent and confident. This type of preparation has been proven effective in countless other professions and situations. Golfers play a hole or an entire course in their heads before they ever pick up a club and race-car drivers run the race track in their minds, hitting every braking point, the apex of every corner and the precise second of every gear change. Let me show you how well it worked in the Clifton case.

Cashing in

I was seated across from Mr. Clifton in his office. I had already sold myself as the agent for the job, exposed the loss, presented my solution, and was now dealing with his objections. Not surprisingly, the first question out of his mouth was, "Why should I buy insurance when I have assets I could sell or borrow against to pay my estate taxes?"

I walked him through my rationale, never stumbling or appearing nervous or concerned. Because of the visualization I had done, I was confident and in control. He nodded in agreement as I presented each of the points to him. In closing I said, "So, borrowing against your assets can actually cost you a lot more than buying insurance. Most people use capital to create interest. What I do is take interest and create all the capital you will ever need, with a greater degree of certainty than a lifetime of planning and hard work."

"You've certainly got an answer for everything."

We ran through a few more of his concerns, all of which I had anticipated, role-played and could answer quickly and effectively. When I left his office that day I carried in my briefcase a signed contract for $12 million worth of insurance. That is the power of visualization.

Strategy 5: Use visualization to solve a megacase crisis

The megacase market is both thrilling and dangerous. Over the long journey from prospect to client, there are many trying moments – moments, when, after months of hard work and positive thinking, the deal crumbles. It's in those moments that I discover what I'm made of.

I do not breeze through megacases undeterred – I have moments of doubt and fear. In those moments, I must decide whether to hang in or walk away. This is an agonizing choice because when I get involved in a megacase I commit my life to it. All the years, the hopes, the dreams are balanced on a knife-edge. But visualization guides me to the right decision.

I visualize both sides of the argument to persist or walk away in the same way I do when I role play prior to sales meetings. In my mind I play out the two scenarios, the pro and the con, and reach a point where the answers become obvious and I am comfortable with the choices I've made.

How I visualize the case to make a decision
When faced with a seemingly insurmountable problem in a megacase, I relax and immerse myself in the case. I let go of all my concerns, let go of all the time and money I have already spent on the case. Then I visualize the conversations I have already had with the prospect or client and their advisors. While I'm replaying that dialogue I try to focus on what the client is really telling me, reaching into their psyche. I try to understand the hidden meaning running underneath what they are actually saying. I ask myself if I have all the facts. I look for small hints or points I may have missed during our meetings or phone calls. Sometimes I spot a hole in the case that I didn't see before because I was in too deep.

In some cases I'll be able to find a creative solution to my problem and will decide to persist with the sale. In other cases I will rerun everything in my head, but not find the hole and then be forced to admit that there is no deal. Either way, visualization is the key. It helps me see the entire battlefield from a wider, more dispassionate perspective. I stop thinking about how much I need or want the sale and therefore I'm fully focused and no longer in danger of making a decision out of desperation. I won't bang my head against the wall when the case is lost just because I want a check, and I won't walk away too soon because I'm sick of the frustration. My goal, when I sit down to visualize is to make a decision that is not based on emotion. I always want to let logic and visualization make my decision.

If I decide the case is a dead-end, I move on and never look back; but if I know it can be salvaged, I figure out the solution and jump in the ring again. For me, no matter what I decide, I find reward in the megacase market. Even if a case never closes, I take what I can from it – everything I learned along the way, all the people I met. And if it does close, I go seeking something bigger.

Something my manager told me

After I closed my first million-dollar policy, my manager said something to me that I will never forget – he said, "David, in all my years in management I have recruited many million-dollar producers but you are the first to come through." I have never forgotten what he said, not because I was the one who had come through, but because his statement revealed a truth I have always believed. The potential to realize our dreams is in all of us.

Five strategies for visualization

1) VISUALIZE YOUR GOALS.

2) PLAN YOUR WORK AND WORK YOUR PLAN.

3) TRAIN YOUR BRAIN FOR SUCCESS.

4) VISUALIZE THE CASE.

5) USE VISUALIZATION TO SOLVE A MEGACASE CRISIS.

I don't consider

my interviews and appointments

with megacase prospects to be

sales meetings, rather

I look at them as auditions

for a role on their

team of advisors.

CHAPTER 11

The mega-agent

To sell megacases, you have to be a mega-agent. A mega-agent should never lose sight of the fact that they are salespeople, but they must be much more than that, they must become trusted financial advisors. When I meet with a prospect, I am really auditioning for a role on their team of advisors. In fact, I see myself as being as valuable to my clients as their CFOs, board members or vice-presidents.

In this chapter, I will show you the two essential strategies I have developed for becoming a mega-agent: 1) Enable your client to make the right decision and 2) Create new knowledge. If you can do those two things well, you will win the trust and business of the most successful people in the country. As you will see in this chapter, I used them to close the biggest case of my life – $140,000,000 worth of insurance.

Strategy 1: Enable your client to make the right decision

If you can enable your clients to make the right decisions, they will welcome you as a member of their team of trusted financial advisors. And to do this, you must commit to delivering the best and most current information. Our age is known as the Information Age, but it should really be known as the Changing Information Age, because the information we learn today will be obsolete tomorrow. This means that before you become a mega-agent, you must first become an 'intelligent agent.'

Become an 'intelligent agent'

I describe myself as an 'intelligent agent,' because part of what I do is deliver filtered information to my clients just like the 'intelligent agents' that Nicholas Negroponte describes in his book, *Being Digital*. His definition of an intelligent agent is a computer program that knows everything you want, everything you like or dislike. This program learns from you as your tastes change over time, so that it is always an accurate reflection of you. These agents are always at work on your behalf. Whether you're sleeping, working or relaxing, your agents are traveling the Internet, searching for information that you want. For instance, if you're a huge soccer fan, your agents would report back to you every time your favorite team scored a goal, won a game or made a trade. Agents can even assemble and deliver to you a personalized newspaper which would be as thick and well-written as the newspaper you received this morning – except it would only contain information that you find interesting. The power of these agents is that, although they are constantly scouring the world for information, they filter out all of the noise, and ensure you are exposed only to the information you have decided you need, saving you time, helping your life and business run more smoothly.

We play a similar role for our prospects. We must first understand our prospects and their needs, scour the world for the right information, then filter it. However, the intelligent insurance agent adds even more value by synthesizing the filtered information into creative solutions. This is the job description of the intelligent agent.

A network of experts

Intelligent life insurance agents enable their clients to make the right decisions, not because they know everything, but because they know how to obtain the necessary information. And they do this by tapping into their network of experts. My own network is one of my greatest value-addeds. By knowing the influential people in the insurance business – the underwriters, actuaries, corporate secretaries, presidents, reinsurers, and the people in the investment side – I am able to deliver the world to my client. And, as you'll see in the following story, I am frequently able to use those contacts to solve the prospect's problem when other agents cannot.

Eating someone else's lunch

One day last year, for example, I was eating lunch with my wife
Teri in a small French restaurant in Toronto. The place was dimly lit,
peaceful and quiet. While we were waiting for our food, a nervous
young man in a black suit was seated at the table next to us. Within
seconds of being seated he began venting huge breaths as if stress
were just erupting from his body. His right knee trembled violently,
rattling the china laid out in front of him.

He ordered a scotch, reached into his jacket and pulled out a
cellular phone. He spoke so loudly it was impossible not to overhear.

"He just won't do it, Ted. The client's ready to buy, he signed
the application, the medical is done, but the underwriter won't
approve it because he says the financial end won't stand up. I can't
believe I finally sold Jonas Donovan $2,000,000 of insurance after
all these years of banging my head against the wall and now my
own company won't insure him.... He owns Blast Co., the diet
shake company, for heaven's sake! He can pay the premiums!
It's only $50,000 a year. Just because his company's private
and he's uncomfortable releasing financial statements...."

The information I had just learned brightened my day considerably.

As soon as I arrived back at my office that afternoon I picked
up a phone book, found the number for Blast Co. and called Jonas
Donovan. When I got him on the phone I said, "Hi, Mr. Donovan,
my name is David Cowper. I'm a life insurance broker. I understand
you need $2,000,000 of life insurance and can't get it placed."

"What?!" he spluttered. "How did you hear about that?"

"Mr. Donovan, when there's 2 million dollars of insurance on
the table, the dogs in the street know about it.... you shouldn't be
worried about how *I* knew about it. However, I do have a solution
to your problem. Would you let me buy you lunch and discuss it
with you?"

Mr. Donovan agreed, and we met the following week. After
thoroughly discussing the problems with the case, I contacted Barry,
an underwriter I knew at one of the larger insurance companies.
Over the years I had brought Barry many interesting and difficult
cases. He was very creative and enjoyed new challenges. We worked
well together, and there was a great deal of mutual respect and trust.

He valued my business, and I valued his expertise. When I discussed the Donovan case, he was eager to tackle it. A couple of months later, Barry and I had arrived at a solution and the case was placed.

Were it not for my strong relationship with Barry, I knew I would have had trouble finding an underwriter willing to devote the time and energy to the case. Obviously the agent in the restaurant did not have a similar relationship with an underwriter.

Advise the client and reveal nothing to anyone else

I should point out that another reason I was awarded that case was that Donovan was incensed that his agent had discussed the details of his case with other people. Although I never mentioned where I had heard about it, Donovan realized that the word was out and it could only have come from one source – his agent. As a trusted advisor, I always keep my counsel. I feel strongly about client confidentiality and I have staked my reputation on it many times. My clients must be able to trust me implicitly. If they can't, they won't tell me what I need to know, and I won't be able to find solutions to their problems.

Make the trend your friend

One effective way of enabling your clients to make the right decisions is by making the trend your friend. But first you must understand what those trends are. I study the news and devour books on economics, politics, tax law, and the future to uncover the trends impacting our business. My library is full of heavily annotated copies of the works of Toffler, Naisbitt, Schumacher, and literally thousands of others. What I learn gives me the confidence to speak about the future of my industry, and sell solutions that work tomorrow as well as today. The following story describes a case I won because I made the trend my friend.

Jack Bohlen

In chapter 9, I told you about the Jack Bohlen case, and said that it had turned out to be a real dogfight. Several agents were bidding for the business, and I had to apply some high-level strategies to ultimately win the case. Here's the story of how I did that.

Jack's accountant, Vince, was a client of mine and someone I had worked with before on other deals. When I got the initial call from Vince to look at the insurance coverage on Jack, he advised me to give Jack what he wanted – the cheapest term insurance I could find. I knew Jack's real insurance need was for his estate and that term was the wrong product. I said no and lost that first round to another agent. But when Jack turned 64 he realized I had been right all along. He called me in to compete for the case because I was the only one who had advised him to convert his term to whole life over all those years. However, the case was complicated and the competition was fierce. To win the business, I had to devise the best possible solution to Jack's estate problem.

For days, I agonized over how I would approach the case. Then, when I had my plan of attack figured out, I arranged a meeting. "Jack," I said, when I sat down across from him to present my first salvo, "I have been thinking about your capital-gains* problem. As I have been saying for years, you need to convert the term you have now to whole life. But what if, in addition to putting whole life in force, we were to arrange that it would pay out on a last-to-die basis?"

"What do you mean?" he asked.

"Let's assume you die before your wife. The government will come in, evaluate all your assets, and calculate your capital gains tax bill based on the gain in those assets. However the estate can elect to defer the tax payment until your wife dies. The tax becomes payable after this second death, and that's when the cash will be needed. With a last-to-die policy the cash will come in when it's needed on the second death, and not before."

"But my wife is in poor health and uninsurable, David," Jack said.

"We can still arrange for a last-to-die policy. The insurance company will simply base the policy on your age and health."

Jack sat silently for a moment thinking over what I had proposed, then lifted his head, looked me in the eye and said, "But now the estate loses the opportunity to invest the death benefit. Why would I want to leave it in the hands of the insurance company and let them earn money on it, when my estate could use it."

"I see your concern, Jack. Why don't you let me discuss it with the insurance company and we'll see if there's anything we can do to satisfy your concern."

"All right, David," Jack said.

---

* THE CAPITAL GAINS TAX IS THE CANADIAN EQUIVALENT OF ESTATE TAXES IN THE U.S.

I hadn't closed the deal, but I did manage to get deeper inside Jack's psyche. I knew he liked the idea of having the death benefit payable the moment taxes were due on the second death. He liked it because it was clean, and because his wife who was infirm wouldn't need to bother reinvesting the funds. But, as a shrewd businessman he wanted to make certain he was getting a good deal. I had to come up with one.

After a couple of days, I found a solution, but because it had never been done before, I needed to get the insurance company on side. I went to them and together we customized a policy for Jack. I was excited and telephoned Jack for another appointment.

Later in the week, I found myself seated in the leather chair in front of Jack's oak desk.

"Jack," I began, "your concern with the last-to-die policy is that the insurance company, not your estate, will benefit from reinvesting the death benefit should you die first."

He nodded.

"I raised that very concern with the insurance company, and they agree that your concern is valid. They are willing to offer the following proposal. In the event that you do die first, the insurance company will notionally pay out the death benefit and reinvest it for you at a rate of return consistent with the Canada Bond rate. In other words, your estate still won't see the money until the second death, but now the death benefit will have grown as though it was invested. So you are not losing any investment opportunity."

"Hmmmm," he said, thinking it over.

To help him along I added, "For example, if your wife outlives you by seven years and the interest rate applied to your death benefit is 10%, your death benefit will grow from $10 million to $20 million tax-free."

"But we could earn more than that 10%."

"But the 10% growth in the insurance plan is tax-sheltered. What you are doing is borrowing the preferred tax status of an insurance company. To match that, you'd have to earn 20% – given a 50% tax rate. Now if you can guarantee that your estate will earn 20% before tax compounded every year, then I wouldn't advise taking my solution."

"I need to talk this over with my accountant," he said.

I left his office empty-handed again. I could feel myself getting closer, but not close enough. I believe any other prospect would have jumped at my solution, but Jack wasn't completely happy.

That evening, while meditating on the case, I realized that Jack wasn't happy with my solution because he didn't believe it was the best solution. He felt there was something missing. It wasn't something he could put his finger on, rather it was an instinct he had. He'd made millions on his instincts, so I decided that he was right – I would have to do better. I stayed up very late that night, going over and over the case in my mind looking for the hole. At around 2:00 AM it hit me – I had been ignoring a very important trend, one that would have dire consequences for Jack's estate. After that I spent another hour figuring out a way to plug the hole.

In the morning I called the insurance company again, and we went back to the drawing board. A few days later I had another proposal for Jack.

I called for another appointment and met Jack early on a Wednesday morning. His face was still, his lips pursed. I could sense that the endless flow of agents in and out of his office over the past few weeks was wearing him down. I decided to go straight for the kill.

"When you die, Jack, the government assesses your tax bill largely on the capital gains tax. Let me quickly take you through an example of how they'll calculate the tax you'll owe. For instance, the Wooler building that you bought in 1971 – it's a commercial property, and if its market value increases as you expect, it will be worth far more when you die than when you purchased it. Say in '71 you paid $1 million, and when you die it's worth $2 million. You've doubled your money. But, now the government wants their share. They step in and apply the capital gains tax. Your capital gain would be $1 million on valuation day. According to the capital gains tax formula, 50% of that would be taxed at the top tax rate of 50%. So your tax bill for Wooler building would be $250,000.

"But the example I just gave you reflects the economic reality ten years ago. Since then the tax has gone up to 66 $^2/_3$% of the gain, and as of last week to 75%.

"Jack, you would now owe $325,000 on that one building. In fact, in the time it has taken us to apply for this insurance and have these meetings, your capital gains tax situation has grown

13 ⅓% worse. Now, you're actually under-insured!"

Jack had been fidgeting in his chair for the past few seconds, then suddenly burst out, "So, what are you saying?"

"Jack, in the future, the capital gains tax in Canada will hit 100%. Everything is pointing to the fact that this increasing trend in capital gains will continue to its ultimate conclusion – a 100% taxable gain. It's the area of tax that still has some room in it. We have too much unemployment, and not enough consumers to make income tax or sales tax a feasible way of raising government revenue. But there is a large number of very sizable estates in this country. And because of the aging population these estates are going to be a veritable gold mine for the government. You think they'll pass up the opportunity to get their hands on our estates in an era of such huge national debt?

"But I have the solution for you. We can build into your policy a clause that states that if the capital gains tax increases before you die, the death benefit will be increased to cover the difference. That way, no matter what the government does your estate will survive intact."

There was a moment's silence. Having made my point and having enough experience to know when to keep quiet, I waited quietly and let Jack think the issues through.

Just before our silence reached its breaking point, Jack reached for the phone on his desk and dialed an internal extension. "Vince, could you come in here for a moment, please? I need to finalize the details of this insurance with Mr. Cowper. Let's cut him the premium check and send him on his way."

Strategy 2: Create new knowledge

Being able to identify the trend in capital gains was only part of the reason I managed to close the Jack Bohlen case. The other part had to do with the fact that I had created a new type of policy. When no product or service currently exists to meet your prospect's needs you must find the solution by creating new knowledge. That's exactly what I did to protect Jack from capital-gains increases, and it's also the second strategy for becoming a mega-agent.

New knowledge: the Substitute Creditor

In my own career, one of the best examples of the power of creating new knowledge is the Substitute Creditor concept. I have referred to this concept in earlier chapters, and promised to tell you about it. Here's how I developed it, and how it led to the $100,000,000 case.

One of my key roles on my client's financial team is underpinning debt. For instance, when a company needs a loan and the bank wants it insured, my clients can call on my services and it then becomes my responsibility to insure that loan, so that the bank doesn't lose their money if my client dies. But, as I said in chapter 3, it's my responsibility to look out for my clients' best interests and it had always bothered me that I wasn't doing that when I insured my clients' loans. In fact, I had always felt I should really be protecting the borrower from the lender, not the other way around. So, a few years ago, I decided to see if there was any way to improve my clients' tax position when I insured the loans they were taking out. I looked at the type of deals being done and how they were being structured and realized that they all had a tragic flaw – but one that could be fixed.

How the Substitute Creditor worked for me

One hot afternoon, about ten years ago, I ate lunch with a very astute and wealthy client of mine at a famous New York restaurant. He was an American and had made his fortune in the auto parts business. Now he was faced with the opportunity to snap up a contract to supply one of the big three automakers with parts from his factories. The only hitch was, he would have to expand his production to meet the demand.

"David," he lamented to me in between courses, "I'm going to have to pledge half my assets to borrow the $20,000,000 to do this retooling. My business needs the cash if it's going to grow and I can't afford to let this opportunity pass us by, but the debt-load is really making me nervous."

"Frank," I replied, "My specialty is underpinning debt, and I have a new plan that we've just developed that would be perfect for this situation. With a traditional insurance plan, when you die the insurance pays off your loan, making it an asset instead of a liability on your company's books. The government would no longer be subtracting the $20 million that you owe from your estate but adding the $20 million that you have brought into the company. That would increase the size of your estate tax bill and in the end cost you more. But, what if I told you, you could increase the cost of borrowing that money by only one quarter of one percent and, in so doing, guarantee that the entire debt be stricken from your books when you die – with no penalty to your estate?"

Frank's fork stopped halfway to his mouth. "What do you mean?" he asked, "Can they do that at the bank?"

"Yes, it's a specialty of ours," I explained. "We work in conjunction with lenders, using our Substitute Creditor concept. We'll structure the insurance so that it's paid out to your wife, Josephine, on your death. The estate taxes will be calculated, including the liability of the unpaid loan, so your company will pay less tax. Then the bank will call their loan, so Josephine, as outlined in the contract, will lend your company $20 million from the death benefit to pay off the loan. Your company pays the bank and then only has to pay Josephine off over time, according to whatever arrangement you want to make. Then she can draw on those funds tax free over the years as she sees fit."

Frank loved the idea and we quickly placed $20 million of insurance with an annual premium of $80,000 to insure their expansion loan. He got the auto contract and his business flourished.

The cycle of new knowledge

The concept of the Substitute Creditor took off soon after I first introduced it to Frank. The truth is you can't trademark an idea, so you're going to have to give it up to the rest of the world at some point. But, the trick is to maximize the headstart you get on the competition. Use your idea in cases as much as you can, and then use the spreading buzz about the idea to give your reputation a boost.

Once the word is out and your secret is uncovered, turn your approach around and instead of trying to jealously guard your idea, promote it aggressively. Once word of the Substitute Creditor concept had begun to spread, I began speaking and writing about it as much as I could. I published articles and contributed to finance books, outlining the key points of the plan. I spoke at conferences and conventions about the value of the plan to clients with large debt-loads. What used to be new knowledge quickly became old knowledge and, in fact, can now be found in basic training manuals. Then the cycle starts again with another piece of new knowledge.

Promoting your knowledge

I owe my $100,000,000 case to my promotion of the Substitute Creditor concept. As I described in chapter 3, after a speaking engagement in Toronto, I was approached by a lawyer who thanked me for my speech and told me he was very intrigued by the idea of the Substitute Creditor. In fact, he had a case he was working on at the moment which seemed ideally suited to an application of it. He suggested I get in touch with another lawyer and that meeting led to the $42,000,000 case, which eventually developed into the $100,000,000 case.

Promoting yourself to the client

The fact that the Substitute Creditor concept led to the $100,000,000 case shows the value of speaking, publishing and teaching every chance you get. I speak all around the world, and also write regular articles in industry papers – because you can't be a famous secret. But it is also important that I promote myself to my prospects and clients.

Let me illustrate how and why I promote myself to my clients by showing you how I closed the biggest deal I ever worked on.

The $140,000,000 case

A few years ago I received a call from an accountant I had worked with previously on many large cases. A client of his was in the market for a massive amount of insurance. I was excited by the size of the case, but knew it would be difficult to close, because there were already other agents competing aggressively for the business. The client was a large privately-held company headed by a group of 7 shareholders. The major shareholder, Anton, essentially ran the company that manufactured home appliances.

At our first meeting, I met with Anton, his accountant, and a couple of the other shareholders to discuss arranging the insurance which would amount to $140,000,000. They needed to finance a buy-out agreement, and so I tabled the concept of a zero-cost option. Anton appeared to support the idea and with his initial approval I spent the next few weeks exploring all the details of the case. Eventually, we all sat down again and I pitched them the final proposal.

Although Anton had been initially bullish about the zero-cost solution, all of the shareholders suddenly developed a case of frostbitten feet. I completely understood their sudden attack of nerves because the economic climate was poor. The cash grab of the late '80s was over and now agents were paying the price for the shady and thoughtless business practices that a few had been promoting five years before. In Canada, one of the major insurance companies and two mid-sized companies had folded. Reports of the impending bankruptcies of several U.S. firms were swirling through the media and there were dozens of class-action suits being brought against both agents and insurance companies because of the poor performances of policies that clients were sold by agents using 'damn-lies' projections. Confidence in the insurance industry had eroded and clients across the country were thinking twice about using insurance to underpin debt because they were scared. Financial officers, accountants and CEOs everywhere were battening down the hatches and making sure that due diligence was being done on each and every case presented to them. As a result, Anton and the other shareholders worked overtime to find any potential problems with the insurance.

I received calls on a weekly basis, from one advisor or another, telling me they had this or that concern with the plan. None of their concerns were new to me because I had used my Process Approach to thoroughly prepare for the biggest case of my life. But the back-and-forth went on so long I knew I had to take it to another level.

Finding the decision maker

At that time I became very concerned that I was not speaking to the decision maker. As I learned early in my career, it's pointless to try and sell an advisor when he will only have to do another – and definitely poorer – sell to the eventual decision maker.

As always, I decided I needed to take the bull by the horns and assume control of the situation, so I began to chase Anton. I knew his concerns were really buying signals and that if he heard a reasonable and well-presented argument that outlined all the logical benefits of the case, his fears would be mollified and I would win the business. As I expected he was initially reluctant to talk to me, but after a few weeks of determined calling, I eventually got him on the phone.

"Anton, it's David Cowper," I said. "I hear from your accountant that you have quite a list of concerns."

"That's right," he said flatly, not offering any further assistance.

"That's great, why don't you fax them over to me so that I can address them and then we'll meet and go over everything."

"All right," he said after a brief pause, "but if I send the concerns to you, I'm sending them to all of the agents."

"Of course, Anton," I said, realizing that he wasn't going to do me any favors.

The next day Anton's list arrived by fax. As I read it over while sitting on the couch in my office, I thought about how I could use these concerns to position myself as the best agent for the case.

The list contained several legitimate and fairly detailed concerns, so my first job was to prepare my answers to those. As I suspected, they were all concerns that I had already thought of, so I wasn't worried about finding the right solutions. However, the other agents were preparing their answers to those same concerns and would have largely similar responses. That meant Anton would have an impossible time trying to decide which one of us would be the most qualified agent for the case.

It would be hard to stand out amongst the competition unless I took my approach to another level. I needed to think like one of his advisors and bring him the information that would enable him to make the right decision about the insurance, whether it ended up being my solution or not. That was a tactic the other agents were unlikely to try, so, encouraged once more, I took a thorough look at the concerns in front of me to see if there were any missing. Carefully, I compared Anton's list to the one I had been compiling over the last five years. His list was excellent, but eventually I discovered that he was missing one crucial concern. It was the edge I had been looking for.

The exception

The next morning I phoned Anton back and said, "I think you've developed a well thought out list of concerns, however, you have overlooked some."

"What do you mean?" he grumbled. "I had my CFO and my lawyers working on those concerns. None of the other agents had any problems."

"Well, let's meet and discuss them then."

He agreed and on the Friday of that week we met in his company boardroom. He sat at the head of the table with the other agents' answers to his concerns placed in front of him. His lawyer, Mr. Marks, was seated to his right.

Patiently, we went through his concerns one by one. I answered each one carefully and with authority as I worked my way down the list – but I saved the biggest, the one that had not been considered, until last. Up to that point he had agreed with my solutions but had been generally unimpressed, it seemed. So the pressure was on.

"Anton," I finally said, "if I were you, my biggest concern with the zero-cost option would be that, no matter what predictions you're hearing about the return on your investment, there really is only one guarantee an agent can make, and that is, whatever figures you look at today will definitely be different tomorrow."

"How do mean?" asked Anton. "Every agent I've had in here has shown me investment forecasts for this policy."

"And did you believe them?" I asked.

Anton looked startled by my question. But, before he could answer, Mr. Marks interrupted, "Mr. Cowper," he asked, "if we went with your policy, would the interest rate that the policy earns always be within two percent of the bank rate? I ask because that's the crucial spread for us, especially if we plan to leverage these policies at the bank one day."

"I see where you're coming from," I replied, "but, remember, the general fluctuation of interest rates could very easily upset your apple cart. If the banks raise their prime rate and the credited rate in your policy is lower than the borrowing rate, you'd be in trouble, particularly if the imbalance continued. The plain truth is, insurance companies cannot react as quickly as banks in dealing with interest rates."

Everybody suddenly looked very uncomfortable. Mr. Marks cleared his throat and then hesitantly said, "Well, your competition told us there was no downside."

I laughed and said, "Mr. Marks, if anyone were to believe that, I could get that person a charter membership in the Flat Earth Society, particularly when dealing with variable interest rates on both sides of the transaction."

Silence followed that statement and, for a few seconds, Anton and his advisors exchanged glances around the table. Finally, after a slight nod from Anton, Mr. Marks stood up and said, "As usual, David, you gave us a very balanced and professional overview with full disclosure – we will get back to you."

That meeting had taken place on Monday. On Friday morning Mr. Marks called on behalf of Anton and said, "You have the case."

Your prospects will look after you

I was glad to hear that Anton and his advisors appreciated my full disclosure, but found it ironic that the biggest case of my life ended with me pointing out a potential problem with my own insurance solution. As life insurance agents, though, we are behooved to disclose all the downsides of the policies we present. I take disclosure very seriously and eagerly disclose everything because, although in our business we don't get paid until a sale is made, my primary goal is to become a part of my prospect's team of financial advisors. As I've said, I don't consider my interviews and appointments with megacase prospects to be sales meetings, rather I look at them as auditions for a role on their team. So I want them to have total confidence in the fact that I have their interests, not mine, at heart, and I am also aware that when I become one of their advisors I will get their business. If you look after your prospects they will ultimately look after you.

Two strategies for becoming a mega-agent

1) ENABLE YOUR CLIENT TO MAKE THE RIGHT DECISION.

2) CREATE NEW KNOWLEDGE.

PART V

Beyond the megacase

By immersing themselves

in the breaking waves of technology

and information,

mega-agents will burst through

the sound barrier,

carrying the industry along

into uncharted territories.

CHAPTER 12

A one-billion-dollar year

I have had a remarkable career in the insurance industry – but my biggest years are still ahead of me. Throughout this book I have shown you how I advanced my career by setting ambitious goals and developing strategies to reach them. Now I have a new challenge – to sell one billion dollars of insurance in one year.

Five business and sales opportunities for the next century

I am optimistic about the possibility of a one-billion-dollar year, because I feel the insurance industry is currently only in its infancy, and is beginning to experience explosive growth as the high-tech revolution moves into overdrive and demographics shift. My plan is to capitalize on 5 opportunities created by these sea changes.

Opportunity 1: The rich are getting richer

The megacase market is the growth market for our business. I say this because advances in technology mean the rich are getting richer. Human beings create technology to make things more efficient. On the shop floor, this means replacing human labor with machines. Human beings demand annual salaries, benefits, can get sick, go on strike, quit, and may not always perform at their peak. Yet machines are purchased once, never get sick, go on strike, or quit, and perform with perfect consistency around the clock. When businesses automate, production costs plummet, profits soar, and the business owners become the beneficiaries of the high-tech revolution. As a result, they will have more wealth to conserve and more credit to underpin, creating fantastic opportunities for insurance agents.

Opportunity 2: The golden age of entrepreneurs

The high-tech revolution is ushering in a golden age of entrepreneurs and creating another fantastic opportunity. The automation of the workplace has catalyzed a frenzy of 'downsizing,' 'rightsizing,' and re-engineering which is flooding the marketplace with terminally unemployed people – many of them skilled, educated and motivated. With their knowledge and experience, these people are starting their own businesses, some in direct competition with their former employers.

Some of these entrepreneurs aren't even waiting to be 'de-hired.' They are leaving of their own accord and taking advantage of the array of high-tech tools – business software packages, telecommunication devices, and the Internet – that allow a single person to run a complicated and lucrative business. Because the barriers to entry are so low, one person can now steal market share from giant multinationals. The huge opportunity for insurance professionals is that this army of entrepreneurs needs benefits, retirement plans, family protection, and business insurance.

Opportunity 3: Knowledge workers

In the high-tech world the knowledge worker predominates. The real value of a company does not lie in its physical assets, but between the ears of its key knowledge workers. A hundred years ago, to be successful in the shoe business all you really required was a factory that could make shoes more cheaply than your competitors. Today, because of automation, all shoe companies can make shoes cheaply. Nike is the number one shoe company in the world, not merely because of its efficient production, but because it creates a new shoe concept everyday and has developed ingenious advertising campaigns that blow its competition away. It owes its success to the knowledge workers responsible for the constant innovation and creativity. Their ideas, not the company's physical assets, are Nike's competitive advantage. And unlike capital and labor, which are finite resources, ideas are inexhaustible. Accountants can no longer place the idea generators – the key knowledge workers – under liabilities as Salaries Paid. Instead, they will have to evaluate these key people as assets – assets that can get sick, die, retire or walk across the street to a competitor. Companies will have nowhere else to turn but to insurance professionals who have always known how to deal with human intellectual capital. We can protect their key assets with golden handcuffs, golden parachutes, and golden handshakes. The opportunities for key person insurance will boom on the heels of the high-tech revolution.

Opportunity 4: The global market

People say, "Think globally and act locally," but I think we should be acting more globally and less locally. The global market is a reality and a great opportunity for the mega-agent because telecommunication makes it easy for us to transact business no matter where our clients are – whether they are in Singapore or Sweden.

Capital has no patriotism and our clients may want to immunize some of their cash holdings against predatory tax collectors and volatile currency markets. To service their needs, we will have to become aware of life insurance products on the global market, where growth can be tax-sheltered and investments made in a variety of currencies. Insurance products will be brought in line with other financial instruments, and will require a much greater degree of sophistication and financial knowledge on our part. If we can master the new knowledge, we will be able to expand our market around the world and thrive in the coming decades.

Opportunity 5: Massive estates

As the North American population ages, we are moving from a society that spends to a society that saves, and opportunities will abound in the estate planning market. The estates we build in our golden years will become the government's new eldorado because, to pay down the annual deficits and national debts that were created by the practice of voodoo economics, governments will have to raid the coffers of the rich. Unless protected by insurance, the estates of the wealthy boomers will be stripped bare before they pass into the hands of their heirs. As insurance brokers armed with eliminate-tax-at-death policies we will preserve what Donald Trump calls 'The Lucky Sperm Club.'

The high-tech revolution and us

Each of us can turn these opportunities into a billion-dollar year because the high-tech revolution is streamlining our business and making us more effective.

The time horizons of an insurance case are collapsing as technology accelerates the underwriting process. I remember when I had to wait a week for a team of number crunchers to produce a quote. Now, we can generate hundreds of quotes on the fly using lightning-fast software packages. Consumers can even create their own quotes on the Internet. When it comes to underwriting at the home office, insurance companies will exploit the advances in artificial intelligence to separate the insurable from the uninsurable. These and other advances mean that both agents and insurance companies will have more time to focus on their clients. We will be creating flexible and highly customized products tailored specifically to meet our clients' needs. We will be able to close deals of extreme complexity and uniqueness that could never have been done previously. By immersing themselves in the breaking waves of technology and information, mega-agents will burst through the sound barrier, carrying the industry along into uncharted territories.

I am excited about my own future in the business, but I know that the bright, young agents coming up behind me will realize dreams far greater than my own.

Five business and sales opportunities for the next century

1) THE RICH ARE GETTING RICHER

2) THE GOLDEN AGE OF ENTREPRENEURS

3) KNOWLEDGE WORKERS

4) THE GLOBAL MARKET

5) MASSIVE ESTATES